...ologist and teacher. Throughout his career he taught in schools and lectured in colleges and universities. He holds a doctorate in education and psychology and has contributed widely to academic books and journals. He is retired and lives with his wife Catherine on the south coast.

Also by Denis O'Connor

Paw Tracks in the Moonlight
Paw Tracks at Owl Cottage
Paw Tracks – A Childhood Memoir

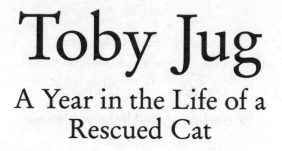

Toby Jug

A Year in the Life of a
Rescued Cat

Denis O'Connor

Constable • London

CONSTABLE

First published in Great Britain in 2014 by Constable

Copyright © Denis O'Connor, 2014

A CIP catalogue record for this book
is available from the British Library.

ISBN 978-1-47211-175-3 (B-format paperback)
ISBN 978-1-47211-176-0 (ebook)

Typeset in Stempel Garamond by TW Typesetting, Plymouth, Devon
Printed and bound in Great Britain by Clays Ltd, St Ives plc

Constable
is an imprint of
Constable & Robinson Ltd
100 Victoria Embankment
London EC4Y 0DY

An Hachette UK Company
www.hachette.co.uk

www.constablerobinson.com

And the souls of whom thou lovest
Walk upon the winds with lightness
P. B. Shelley
'Hymn to the Spirit of Nature'

I dedicate this book to cats everywhere

CONTENTS

A Festive Christmas   1

The Private Life of Toby Jug   31

Toby Jug and a Horse Called Lady May   43

A Camping Adventure and a Sad Loss   72

All at Sea   100

The Raven and the Witch of Rampton Hall   115

Toby, Fynn and the Otter Hunt   137

The Menace of the Hornets' Nest   160

Sojourn with a Pony Trap   180

Perspectives   198

A FESTIVE CHRISTMAS

It was after midnight as I lay awake in Owl Cottage. All was calm and still now the wind had dropped. Lower down the bed, under the patchwork quilt, I could feel the body of Toby Jug, my three-year-old Maine Coon cat, lying across my ankles and warming my feet like a hot-water bottle. This was his preferred sleeping position during cold weather.

It was the third week in December 1968 and Alnwick College, where I taught, was closed for the Christmas break, which meant that I was on holiday until early January. It had been a term of hard work and I was exhausted, but that night I could not sleep. Reaching out, I drew back the curtains at the bedside window to look out on the garden and watched as a silver half-moon cast pale shadows between the trees. Nothing stirred, but earlier I'd heard the cries of a little owl from an adjacent copse.

Pangs of hunger drove me downstairs to the kitchen where I prepared a quick snack of a corned beef sandwich lathered in mustard and a hot mug of Earl Grey tea to wash it down. At the side of my plate I left a thin slice of meat without mustard for my erstwhile companion who, sure enough, appeared just as I poked the sitting-room fire back into life. Wherever I went Toby Jug followed, if he could, and in the cottage we were inseparable. Wrapping a woollen rug around my shoulders, I snuggled into the armchair by the fire and prepared to enjoy the midnight feast. Meanwhile, a sleepy-eyed cat scrambled onto the arm of the chair and stared intently at me. As usual I felt obliged to offer an explanation.

'I just couldn't sleep, Toby, and I was so hungry. Sorry I woke you but I've made you a tasty bite.'

I turned my plate in his direction so he could reach the proffered morsel of corned beef. He yawned twice to let me know that getting up in the middle of the night, except in an emergency, required quite some effort even for a nocturnally minded creature like himself. He accepted the refreshment as recompense for his trouble.

As the fire blazed we happily ate our food and I drank my brew. Soon after, comforted by the warmth and the food, I started to drift off with a black and white cat purring contentedly on my lap. As sleep started to catch hold of me, memories of this little cat, some good, some frightening, slipped into my mind – including the terrible night when I tracked across the fields to find a soon to be orphaned kitten. I nursed that kitten back to health, and, from that day on, Toby Jug and I had shared great adventures together.

We were both still young, and in many ways we were both still finding our feet in the world. I was looking forward to the year ahead, wondering what new adventures the next twelve months and the changing of the seasons would bring. Little did I know, as I stroked Toby's fur and sleep gently took full hold of us both, quite what a year 1969 was going to turn out to be. I would remember it forever.

I awoke slowly, soothed by the serenity of the old cottage. This was the home I had chosen when I was appointed to a lectureship at Alnwick College of Education. The cottage in the village of West Thirston was stone built and dated from the beginning of the eighteenth century. Its massively thick walls and old-fashioned construction gave it a quaint, rustic appearance that I had found irresistibly appealing. It was just what I'd always dreamed of having as my home someday. It was cool in summer but warm in winter, especially when the open log fire was burning. The view from each window looked out onto a landscape of trees and flowering bushes. I loved the place – it was my Shangri-la.

Suddenly I had an urge to go for a walk and refresh my tired mind. It was still dark outside but daylight could not be far off and it would do my heart good to savour the freedom of the break from work. As I dressed, Toby Jug ran into the small kitchen and whined for his breakfast.

'We'll eat later,' I told him, 'after our walk.'

He was not impressed by this and kept nudging my leg with his head to indicate that he wanted his food now. Looking down at his sturdy little form, I felt again the deep attachment I had for this beloved cat of mine. Relenting somewhat, I placed a small handful of dry biscuits in the feeding bowl.

'There now,' I said. 'Let that suffice till we get back.' This did not go down at all well.

As I slipped into my sheepskin jacket and reached for my walking stick, Toby, still chewing on a mouthful of biscuits, rushed to the door eager not to be left behind. From a coat hook I took down his harness and lead – I didn't want him running off into danger in the dark. On leaving the cottage I heard the French clock on the mantelpiece chime six o'clock. The ancient timepiece was a much-valued memento from my maternal grandmother and I lovingly wound its delicate mechanism every week.

A hoar frost covered the ground and the earth crunched under my feet. Toby Jug padded along at my side, seemingly as happy as I was to be out in the fresh, frosty air. Now and again he would pull off to one side as he scented something worth investigating, but just for now, for caution's sake, I kept him on a tight lead. As we skirted the old donkey meadow at Willowbrook Farm I could see ahead the inky black mass of Stag Wood looming on the horizon.

Moonlight had lit the path but the sun was now rising to unveil our surroundings. We stopped for a breather by the cattle grid and I leaned on the stile. Toby Jug jumped up beside me and whined to my face, causing me to chuckle at his impatience to carry on with our walk.

The sky was now beginning to brighten. Strands of dawn light crept along the ground and faintly illuminated the ragged grasses and thorn bushes lining the woodland edge. The scene was rapidly changing as the wild terrain became clearer with every passing minute. A seeping glow invaded the woodland, giving rise to a trace of birdsong that all at once swelled to a chorus of trills and warbles. We stood together, cat and man, enchanted by the experience. Nothing, I thought, surpasses the charm bestowed by an English wood, whatever the season.

With our spirits uplifted, we moved deeper into the forest. Tendrils of mist from the damp ground encircled the tree trunks, and foraging shrews and roe deer roused to meet the demands of a winter's day. We came upon open patches where there was still some grass toned with a frosty sheen like green silk. This was the domain of the rabbits whose burrows had tunnelled an age-old living space underground. Today they were out en masse, feeding early, a sure sign that rain was due, and the pregnant does amongst the rabbits had pressing appetites.

Vigilant bucks were on guard, keeping a wary lookout for badger and fox, but they were not alarmed as we passed by at a safe distance. Toby Jug tugged at the lead, moved by a desire to join them, but I kept him tied firmly to hand, remembering how he'd once, to my dismay, chased some rabbits down a burrow.

Eventually the morning sunbeams were eclipsed by darkening clouds. As we continued our walk the onset of rain intermingled with icy sleet dampened the ground, which prompted Toby Jug to stop and shake his paws in irritation. We lingered by a high stand of willows that afforded us some shelter under their canopy of leaves. Bubbling springwater fed the pool nearby. Here in summer dippers dived for beetle larvae amid streaks of turquoise and crimson as kingfishers plunged for minnows. In spring, crested newts in the depths of the pond would flash their mating colours of vermilion and black stripes, but today these miniature dragons were nowhere to be seen. The pool was beginning to freeze over as Toby Jug and I stared down into its depths.

Toby was starting to look bedraggled in the rain and wasn't happy about the situation.

'Time to turn back and go home, Toby,' I said, and received what I took to be a thankful glance from my cat.

As we returned we passed through a plantation of pines and firs where deer often rested and concealed their fawns. A red squirrel, startled at our intrusion, chittered angrily at us from on high. We pressed on with thoughts of breakfast and the comforts of home. Toby Jug, ignoring the protestations of the squirrel, led the way, head down, and ploughed on like the gutsy little fellow he was.

Soon we came in sight of the cottage and I let Toby's lead loose so that he could race ahead. When I reached the door he was perched on the windowsill giving himself a preliminary tongue-wash to deal with his saturated fur.

Once inside the cottage, I picked up the rain-soaked cat and, placing him on the kitchen bench, gave him a thorough rub down with a thick towel I kept for his use alone. He soon resembled a fluffy ball of fur. He was a fine-looking, healthy cat, mostly black with a skewed white dab on his face, which gave him a quizzical expression. His chest had a large patch of white fur that extended under his chin. All four paws ended in white socks which could be mistaken for spats and gave him the dapper look of the dandy. Dry and clean once more, he looked a real 'Bobby Dazzler' as he jumped down, anxious for a feed.

I heated some gold-top milk, full of Jersey cream, in a small saucepan. Next I broke a plain digestive biscuit in half and placed the crumbs in Toby's dish. Adding the warm milk would give him a delicious treat such as he used to have when he was a sickly kitten. The rest of the milk would go into my hot coffee. Opening a cupboard, I took an unopened bottle of five-star brandy, a present from the staff of the college at our end-of-term Christmas party. A generous dollop of the golden spirit in my coffee would do wonders to restore inner warmth after the bracing walk in the woods.

Meanwhile, Toby Jug began to sing, or else purr loudly, as he gobbled his milky pick-me-up. As I listened to his engaging song I thought that singing was just what was required. Tonight, after dinner, I'd play some Verdi to liven up the evening.

Now I had a log fire to prepare and candles, lots of candles, to set around the parlour with its arched stone fireplace and inset iron oven with stone ledges for pots and pans. When the fire took hold, its blazing heat would permeate the whole cottage and render the place snug and warm. Afterwards I would prepare a pan of Northumbrian vegetable broth made with barley, leeks, onions, carrots and as many other vegetables, including potatoes and red lentils, as I could find from my garden store. I'd then cook it slowly on the stone ledge at the side of the open fire. Six hours of simmering heat would turn the broth into a classic life-saver.

As I carried out these chores I was amused to see Toby Jug playing a vigorous game of pawball with one of his favourite red balls, and I recalled the incident of the neighbour's stolen tomatoes, which he mistook for red balls during his first year of life.

'Oh well, a cat must do what a cat must do; no question of that where Toby Jug's concerned!' I mused to myself. In the meantime, I determined to hunt out some of the Christmas decorations I'd stored away in the loft last year.

Tomorrow I'd go shopping in Morpeth and see if I could buy a small fir tree. I also needed to collect holly and ivy from the garden to give the cottage a seasonal look. With a decorated Christmas tree adorning the space in front of the patio door, a streamer of multicoloured lights hanging above the fireplace and a multitude of candles everywhere, plus a pot of broth bubbling alongside the fire, the cottage would have a cosy festive atmosphere. All that was needed was a large goose and a supply of mince pies. For good measure I would fish out my copy of Dickens's *A Christmas Carol* to re-read by the fire and my celebration would be complete.

Outside the sky was darkening, but still the bird feeder hanging by the window was in huge demand by the blue tits and goldfinches, together with a motley collection of ravenous sparrows, robin redbreasts and a nuthatch. They all relied on me for their daily feed of seeds and peanuts. Toby Jug, however, did not approve. He made rattling noises with his teeth and whined whenever he caught sight of the birds through the window.

A sudden noise by the back door alerted my attention. Toby Jug heard it too and ceased his game to stare towards the hallway. When I opened the door there was a plump hare hanging from the door handle. A movement in the garden caught my eye and I saw a retreating figure wearing a cap and scarf, accompanied by a lean black lurcher. I knew at once who'd left the game: Tom and his dog.

We hardly ever met and even less rarely talked, but he accepted me as someone who minded his own business. Our acquaintance began one night when I was taking a walk with Toby Jug. We were down by the bank of the Coquet River when I came across a man catching salmon in the shallows with a hooked tool called a gaff. He was knee-deep in the river and in plain sight. We made eye contact as I walked by and I bade him goodnight abruptly, anxious to exit the scene.

I realized on reflection that he would have been worried that I would report him to the Water Bailiff for illegal fishing: if convicted, a heavy fine and possibly a prison sentence would follow. Salmon fishing earned big money and the stock was the monopoly of the landowner – the Duke of Northumberland. I had no intention of reporting the fisherman, as age-old country practices like a spot of poaching add to the flavour of a community.

Since then, whenever we met he treated me with marked respect. He had obviously found out my name and greeted me as 'Doc', probably because of my initials rather than my university doctorate. He once told me that his name was Tom and that he lived alone in a cottage in the woods and did odd handyman jobs around the village. Occasionally he would leave me a trout or a brace of quail as a friendly gesture, hence the hare tonight. In spring he often left me half a dozen double-yolked pheasant eggs he got from his brother, who worked on the Duke's estate. The eggs made delicious omelettes.

Respect and trust, once it is earned in a small village, is never forgotten. I decided to hang the hare in my cold pantry and in the New Year we'd have jugged hare for dinner, thanks to Tom and his dog.

Next morning I set off in the car on my shopping trip. To his disappointment I didn't take Toby with me since I expected that some of the things I wanted would necessitate a further journey to Newcastle upon Tyne. As I drove away I could see my cat in the rear-view mirror straddled high in the old apple tree branches, watching the car disappearing up the road. I knew that whenever I left he missed me, but I trusted that he understood I would return. I'd make it up to him tonight but I didn't feel that he would be safe alone in a car parked in the city.

Shopping a few days before Christmas is always a hectic affair but I have to admit that I'm addicted to the festive mood created by Christmas lights and the sound of the carols – a morale booster in the face of harsh weather.

After a full day at the shops I was ready for home. I'd bought a large oven-ready goose from a poultry trader in the Grainger Market. Since I had recently been promoted to Head of Department I could afford to be indulgent so I also bought several presents for the cottage, chiefly coloured candles and some long-playing records of classical music. Sheila Nutley, head of music at the college, had given me a recording of Tchaikovsky's ballet music for Christmas to balance what she considered to be my 'macho' personality. I intended to impress her with my knowledge of opera next term.

Also, I had a secret. In one of the high cupboards in the kitchen, which I had at last got around to cleaning, I found a tattered recipe book from the mid-eighteenth century which described how best to cook a goose in traditional Old English fashion. I decided to cook my goose using this method. As the recipe required some additional items that I hadn't been able to get in Newcastle, I would have to make a special trip to Rothbury, which allegedly had one of the best butcher's shops in the world. I was sure they would have what I needed and Toby would love making the trip too.

Toby Jug appeared in the driveway as if by magic as soon as the car returned. He felt that he had to sniff each and every one of the parcels as I carried them into the cottage. The ancient goose recipe had fired my imagination and I wanted to copy the way others in the past had celebrated Christmas in my cottage. The notion had an exciting, Dickensian quality about it.

I gave Toby Jug a plate of chicken livers while I had a welcome mug of tea and an egg-and-cress sandwich. Then I set about the preparations I had in mind. First of all, I lit the fire and, as the firewood and the logs took hold, I could not resist kneeling in front of it for a few moments to relish the luxuriant heat. The ancient stone fireplace was my only form of heating, except a single-bar electric fire, and it was the soul of our cottage. I say 'our' because in all respects Toby Jug shared my life here and his lively presence had turned the cottage into a home. Having finished his dinner, he now joined me and our faces glowed in the firelight.

Sometime later I had assembled enough bric-a-brac to engender the yuletide spirit I had planned. The small tree, set firmly in its container, was placed in prime position in front of the glass patio door. I persuaded myself that a string of sparkling tinsel and a few glass baubles gave the tree an elegant look. I hoped it would survive indoors for a couple of weeks so that I could later plant it in the garden.

Then I started to prepare the mixture for a broth and when it was ready I poured it into a pot-bellied pan, which I put at the side of the fire to cook slowly. I had discovered this iron pot, whose shape resembled a witches' cauldron, when I was clearing out the woodshed. It now held pride of place by the fire and had served up some magnificent stews. Furthermore, the broth when ready would serve many days as a pick-me-up, especially if the weather worsened, which was more than likely. Next I arranged the candles around the room.

Then I cooked a thick steak with potato mash and peas for my own dinner, but whilst I was eating Toby performed his usual begging act and was not content until I'd cut him a thin slice of steak, a simple enough gesture as a token of my love for him. I made a pretence of criticizing him for being greedy but it was very much tongue-in-cheek. In his mind, what was good for me must also be good for him, a policy from which he never deviated. After all, I was the only family he knew and he hadn't had a mother cat as role model. Everything I did was a learning curve for his maturing personality. I was everything to him because he had known nobody else in his life as a kitten.

Relaxing in the armchair by the fireside, I was at last able to appreciate my efforts to create an atmosphere of snug comfort in the room. The warming red glow from the fire and the soft light from the candles created an old-world enchantment. Last night I had gone to bed early to catch up on sleep, but tonight I meant to play some opera. I'd chosen a recording of Verdi's *Rigoletto*. As the music swelled around me, Toby Jug dozed by the hearth.

After the music finished, the melodies were still resounding in my head and I couldn't bear to switch on my tiny radio. Turning on the radio only to hear repeated reports of doom and gloom was fast becoming an aversion to me. This might have been a residue from my childhood experiences during the Second World War when people were terrified at the prospect of listening to yet more bad news on the radio.

There were many such comfy occasions to be enjoyed in Owl Cottage during the winters that Toby Jug was there with me. As the turn of the year approached, I knew that the memory of a certain snow-filled night in January 1966 would come to mind. I would never forget the traumatic events of that night when I had rescued the silver she-cat and her two kittens. That night a barely alive, minute creature had entered my life and changed it forever.

The next day we set off on the twisting rural roads for Rothbury. Despite the weather, which was raw and damp, the drive was pleasant especially when the sun appeared,

albeit infrequently. The butcher's was crammed with customers, but eventually it was my turn to be served and
I was not disappointed. I purchased just what I wanted,
fresh from the extensive cold store: a large cockerel and
a plump partridge, complete with feathers, and for good
measure half a dozen links of venison sausage and a jar of
duck fat.

Returning to the car with a heavy bag full to the brim,
I sent Toby into wild gyrations of excitement, but I had
one more call to make that would please him even more:
to buy fish and chips for lunch. I parked by the river and
we shared the spoils: he had a fried fish with the batter
removed whilst I ate the rest supplemented with tasty
mushy peas. Meanwhile, we watched the swans and the
ducks on the river and I caught a glimpse of a water vole
angling through the reed beds.

On the drive home I became aware that there was
going to be a change in the weather. There was no sunshine anymore – just scudding clouds and a fierce wind
stripping the trees of their remaining leaves and scattering twigs across the road. As we drew nearer home it
began to snow heavily, and when I stepped from the car
a flock of rooks flew in cackling chorus across the darkening sky to their rookery among the pine trees just
across the road from our garden. The view out towards
Cheviot was fast becoming obscured but I could still
discern the summit coated white with snow before the
weather drove us indoors. I paused by the conservatory
window simply to gaze at the scene unfolding outside.
Toby jumped onto the windowsill and we both stared

mesmerized as the snowfall created a frosted wilderness in our garden. I recalled the remarkable fact from a school physics lesson that each snowflake has a unique shape and size, just one of the marvels of nature.

'Isn't it wonderful?' I said, and Toby wagged his tail in affirmation. There is something quite special, even for a cat, about witnessing the first snowfall of winter.

Once inside the cottage we huddled by the fire, which I poked alive, and then I noticed for the first time this winter that both Toby Jug and I were shivering with the chill. No doubt a foretaste of things to come. Still, the trip today had proved most successful and tomorrow Toby Jug would find the plucking and cleaning of the fowl an enthralling experience. I hoped I would, too, as I'd never done anything like it before. When I examined the yellowed pages of the age-old recipe again, I noticed in faded writing the title 'Jacobean Christmas Fayre'. I was sure that if all went well my cat and I were in for a real treat.

I decided that I would pluck the birds outside on the patio to the side of the conservatory, which would be clear of snow since there was a roof overhang. It was sure to be a messy business and I didn't want feathers all over the house. Of course, I also realized that a possible disruptive factor in these proceedings would be Toby Jug. In this respect I was not mistaken, but I did underestimate the amount of chaos his behaviour would cause.

The next morning I took a small wooden stool outside and placed the two fowl, ready for plucking, on the garden wall at my side. Toby Jug was all amazement, not being sure what to expect. As soon as I started to pluck the birds he began to play chase the feathers. Soon, the pile of feathers grew, causing him to indulge in a manic phase of repeatedly charging the growing mound and then pouncing on individual clumps. In no time at all he had feathers in his mouth, feathers stuck to his paws and eventually feathers covering every inch of his body as he rolled around in an ecstasy of playtime. It was impossible to restrain him.

Then came the downside. He began to sneeze and cough and finally developed a choking fit because some feathers had got into his throat. Grabbing him by the scruff of the neck, I put two fingers in his mouth and quickly began fishing out tufts of feathery bits that were blocking his airway.

'Silly little cat. What are you?'

He was in a right mess and soaked to the skin with rolling about in the snow. The only recourse I could think of, now his mouth was clear, was to take him inside for a good brush and a warm bath. I filled the large stone kitchen sink with warm water and a drop of mild shampoo, plonked him in and gave him a thorough bathe.

It took two large towels to dry him and then I used a hair-dryer on a low setting. Even so, he hated the blasts of hot air on his body. Over an hour later I was able to resume my job with the fowl, only to be subjected to repeated wails from a cat glued to the kitchen window, desperate to be out again.

I spent three hours plucking and cleaning the birds but eventually they were ready for the pot. I swept the feathers into a bucket which I stored in the woodshed – in the spring I would put the pail out for the garden birds to help themselves to nesting material.

Toby Jug was in a huff because I'd shut him inside most of the afternoon, but once the fire was burning and the food was being prepared he brightened up and became his old affable self. I took time out to stroke and fondle him just so he would know that things were all right between us.

We ate supper in front of the log fire which, together with a full stomach, is an irresistible precursor to the need for sleep. It had been an eventful day and we were both tired. Tomorrow would be Christmas Eve and I would prepare the birds for the oven. I left the pot of broth bubbling away as I mounted the stairs, preceded by the little lord himself, and soon Toby and I were both happily tucked away in dreamland.

I awoke to the sound of scratching at the bedroom window. It was Toby Jug trying to see through the frosted window panes. Sometimes he was able to lick a patch clear, but the frost was too hard for him this morning. The temperature had fallen steeply during the night and frost had covered every window in the cottage except in the sitting room where the fire still gave off some heat.

I dressed quickly in the cold bedroom, adding a thick woollen sweater on top of a thin roll-neck jumper made of lamb's wool and a vest. The Northumbrian climate necessitates lots of insulation during wintertime, especially in a cottage with no central heating.

Reviving the fire was easy since a first rake revealed lots of red embers. Before banking it with logs I tipped three shovels of coal onto some sticks. When it took hold I pulled back the grate and pushed hot coals under the huge fireside oven where I would cook the birds. The small electric oven in the kitchen was not big enough for the goose and also I wanted to cook the Christmas meal in the traditional cottage way using the same method as the people living here before me. Piling on the hardwood logs, I soon had a mighty hot blaze defrosting the cottage.

Whilst I was busy with the fire, Toby Jug was harassing me for his breakfast, which was number one priority on his agenda. I did my best to ignore him, as I intended to cook a panful of venison sausages with fried bread later. After a while he stopped wailing but he followed me everywhere, just in case I sneaked away to eat breakfast without him.

In a short while the cottage felt a lot warmer and I decided to listen to a recording of Christmas carols sung by the University Choir at King's College, Cambridge. One of my favourite carols, 'In the Bleak Midwinter', was playing as I fried the sausages in duck fat, essential to bring out the venison flavour. Outside in the garden the scene was a polar landscape, with finches and sparrows mounting a feeding frenzy at the bird feeders despite the frequent showers of snow.

We ate breakfast on the small table in the kitchen. Toby Jug had two sausages which I'd cut into thin pieces in his dish for him at the opposite side of the table. This was how we had our meals during the times when I did not have to rush off to college. It was a familiar setting for us, but I suppose a visitor might have found this somewhat bizarre.

I had four sausages and two buns cut in half and fried in the duck fat until crisp. A half-pint mug of Earl Grey tea made the meal complete. As I cleared away our dishes Toby took a prowl outside to do his business and I took advantage of his absence to dress the birds for cooking.

Having washed the three birds thoroughly inside and out, I followed the instructions in the ragged recipe book and carefully inserted the partridge inside the body cavity of the cockerel. I then sealed the cavity with cocktail sticks pierced through the loose skin. Next I cut a lemon in half and rubbed the cockerel all over with the juice to soften the skin. After this I packed the cockerel carcass inside the goose and again sealed the cavity. The birds were now ready for the oven.

After placing the goose inside a large roasting tin I arranged some potatoes around the sides. I knew that once the goose started cooking the fat would stream down and cover everything. Then I put an assortment of vegetables – carrots, Brussels sprouts and parsnips, together with some broad beans I'd saved from the autumn harvest – into a covered iron pan and covered them with salted water. I hadn't bothered with a Christmas pudding but instead I'd bought a sherry trifle from the store in the village. So with my seasonal repast all set and sorted, I could at last relax. Tonight, I thought, I'd have a bowl of broth and Toby could have the remnants of the chicken livers from the fridge.

Suddenly I became aware of a distinctive series of wails from outdoors, which could only be my beloved cat back from roaming. By this time it was the middle of the afternoon and the sky was darkening. As I let Toby inside, I searched the horizon for a sunset but couldn't find even a trace of orange or red. I fed the fire with logs and coal to make sure the oven would be hot enough next morning to cook the meal. Time to light the candles and drink a glass of full-bodied Merlot to toast the yuletide spirits and then listen to Puccini's opera, *Madame Butterfly*.

It was whilst the Humming Chorus was playing that I became aware that Toby Jug was purring loudly along with the music. Puccini had been inspired to compose this particular piece of music whilst watching the green shoots of reeds swaying and wavering in the breeze, and Toby obviously thought he had done a good job. Loud purring resumed at the height of the soprano's aria 'One Fine Day', a favourite piece of mine. Perhaps the music reminded Toby of the natural habitats he loved to explore, or maybe he was just an exceptionally musical cat. I felt really proud of him and made up my mind to tell him so later.

As the soprano's voice grew higher I found myself, not for the first time with Puccini's music, beginning to weep with the sheer emotion of it all. Then something remarkable happened. Toby Jug, sensitive to my feelings, crawled from his place on my lap to my shoulder and lovingly licked the tears from my cheek. Was there ever such a cat as him? Was there ever such an animal friend? Surely it could only have been an act of providence that brought him into my life, or so I liked to believe. I was overwhelmed with affection for him and made a real fuss of him there and then.

When the opera had finished I sat awhile to allow the music to settle in my mind. Much later I returned to reading *A Christmas Carol* and lost myself in the aura of a Victorian Christmas. I had only been reading for half an hour when there came a loud knocking at the front door of the cottage.

I didn't mind the intrusion at all since I had been expecting this visit. It was the choir from St Michael's Church in Felton along with some children from the village primary school, collecting for the homeless. I ushered them round to the back of the cottage in front of the conservatory in which I had laid out some mince pies and chocolate biscuits. For the adults I'd prepared a ginger wine punch and for the children a pitcher of home-made lemonade, which I'd made with fresh lemons, using my grandmother's recipe.

The choir grouped outside in the frosty air, their traditional candlelit lanterns hanging from poles with a bent hook at the top, and they sang a selection of popular carols. Meanwhile, Toby Jug, ever the socialite, frisked among the singers gaining random strokes here and there. Their sweet-voiced singing was a delight to hear, but the final carol, 'Silent Night', was especially moving since, just as the choir began to sing, it started to snow ever so gently, the slowly drifting flakes endowing a sense of spiritual awe to the carol.

The experience gave me a Christmas memory I shall never forget. I put two half crowns in their collection box because it was the best amateur performance I had ever heard and worth every penny. I invited them into the warmth of the conservatory and they helped themselves to the goodies and we wished each other a Merry Christmas and a Happy New Year.

Then all at once they were on their way and I stayed at

the door of the conservatory a little while longer to listen to the strains of their singing further up the village. Soon the icy air had me shivering, as was my cat, who dutifully remained at my heels until I decided to return inside. It had proved an exceptional day and I was looking forward to tomorrow.

I awoke early, feeling excited about the coming festivities, and got up at once. The bedroom felt piercingly cold with frozen, frosted windows once again, and I was glad to go downstairs. The fire was still hot and I soon had a blaze going, which meant that I could start cooking in a short while. I made my morning brew of tea and a slice of toast covered in thick marmalade, and yet still Toby Jug hadn't appeared. No sooner had I thought that than Toby walked in and warmed himself in front of the fire while having a quick freshen up with a tongue-wash.

'Thought you'd have a lie-in, did you?' I asked.

He looked at me as if to say, 'Well, it is still dark and, anyway, it's only six o'clock. What's the rush?'

I always talk to the animals and birds in my life as if they know what I am saying. In the case of Toby Jug I was a hundred per cent sure that he not only understood what I said to him but could sometimes read my mind. Similarly, I felt that I could read his.

I was planning a surprise morning trip but I wasn't ready to tell him about it yet. Urgency demanded that I check the oven, which I found to be roasting hot. Delighted, I took the roasting pan loaded with the prepared fowl and slid it into the hot oven, firmly closing the heavy iron door. I could imagine everything would be sizzling away in no time at all.

Now for the surprise trip – but only after His Majesty had reluctantly made do with a handful of dry biscuits. The trip I had in mind was a visit to the old church at Felton. I knew that there wouldn't be a service until later in the day but I felt a need on this special day to express, on my own, a spiritual feeling which was of ultra importance to me. It seemed an appropriate time of the year to review my life situation. I was in philosophical mood as I reflected on my circumstances and that I was presently having it so good. I have long believed in the dictum of 'savouring the moment'. For the last three years I had been truly fortunate to be gifted with the cat I called Toby Jug. How long I would have him was out of my hands, but on this Christmas morning I wished to visit a place of worship and give thanks.

I drove up to the church gates and parked just as the first red streaks of dawn were lighting the sky. Toby joined me from the car as I unlatched the gate and walked up the snow-covered path to the porch. The heavy door was closed and locked but I'd anticipated that. I sat down on the stone bench by the side of the porch and called Toby Jug to come to me. Lifting him on my knee, I bowed my head in meditation and said a silent prayer of thanksgiving. It took only a moment, but afterwards I felt so much better. I didn't know then how strange and sometimes tough the year ahead would be, and that by the end of it I would be even more grateful to have Toby at my side.

Later Toby and I walked around to the back of St

Michael's Church, where there was a grassed area with trees and, as I had expected, the birds were beginning to appear with the dawn. I spread some crusts I'd saved for the visit and enjoyed watching the blackbirds and the other songbirds enjoying the snack. When I looked down I could see Toby psyching himself up to charge at them, a ploy he enjoyed for no other reason than he liked to scatter them aloft again, when suddenly two magpies arrived and began strutting around, boldly dominating the food. Toby Jug then had second thoughts and decided discretion was the better part of valour. He studiously ignored the magpies until one of them approached too close for comfort, making him seek refuge behind my legs.

'Things never change,' I said to myself, remembering how on his first Christmas he reacted to the presence of some ducks we went to feed at Bolam Lake by hiding behind me, which for him was the safest place in the world. I walked around to the front and stood on the pathway leading to the porch. The ancient stone church building had an elegance about it coupled with an aura of mysticism. I looked around for a while and savoured the moment.

'Time to go home,' I said, and together we returned to the car with my mission completed.

It was cold in the car so it was a relief to once again feel the cosy heat of the cottage. The fire was a roaring mass of blazing logs, and delicious cooking smells were circulating everywhere. Toby Jug, after initially warming himself, began to pad around in circles with his nose held high in the air and his eyes half closed to better relish the exotic aromas. I chuckled as I watched him moved to ecstasy when I opened the oven door to baste the goose. It was coming along very well and I ladled off some goose fat into a stone storage jar before returning the pan to the oven.

Well satisfied with developments, I played carols to enhance the festive feeling. I reckoned the goose would take another two hours before it was ready to eat and in the meantime I would sit in the conservatory and watch the snow and the birds ravaging the feeders I'd refilled with peanuts and suet pellets. I found this very relaxing, but Toby refused to leave the vicinity of the oven and the enticing fragrance of the cooking. But then he was always something of a 'Cold Harry' and could tolerate being very close to the fire much more than I could. With the added incentive of the cooking smells, proximity to the fireside was irresistible to him.

As time went by I judged the goose would be almost done, and on checking the vegetables I found them to be deliciously hot and ready for eating. I left the goose to cool a little before attempting to carve it, but the sight and smell of it was so overpowering that I just couldn't wait and had to launch into the carving. I cut two large slices of the succulent dark meat for me and one for Toby Jug. But surprise, surprise, he wouldn't eat it. Perhaps the colour and taste of the dark flesh did not match the appeal of turkey and chicken, so instead I cut him two slices of the white cockerel meat which I had intended to keep only for cold suppers and sandwiches.

The hot fat from the goose had rendered the chicken

and partridge flesh into tender, choice meats flowing with juices, which must have been the intention of the ancient recipe. The whole meal was a great success and we both had second helpings of our preferred cuts. Afterwards, with our stomachs full, it was time for an afternoon snooze in front of the fire.

Much later, in the evening, I opened our presents, including a new, deep cushion bed for Toby Jug and several packets of treats which I was certain would be greatly appreciated. I received a thick woollen sweater from my mother and a bottle of green Chartreuse, a liqueur comprising vintage brandy and aromatic herbs made by the Carthusian monks at a French monastery. The bottle was from Madeleine – Maddy – my current girlfriend, who was away on a year's secondment at an American college.

Before retiring for the night I made myself a tasty sandwich of goose laced with hot mustard and a mug of creamed coffee with a glass of Maddy's Chartreuse; Toby had some chicken and a saucer of warm milk to which I'd added the contents of a halibut oil capsule to keep him healthy. I banked up the fire with coal to last till morning and then we were off to bed.

It had been a super Christmas in which I'd tried new things and once again enjoyed my time in the cottage with Toby Jug, whose presence in my private world banished any feelings of loneliness I might otherwise have had. During the next few days I would return to my writing since there was a strong likelihood that we would be snowed in, but there was plenty of food and I hadn't arranged to go anywhere in particular.

The forecast proved to be accurate and for the next week we experienced severe weather conditions with icy temperatures and lots of snow. I did venture out on a few short walks with Toby Jug just for the fresh air and the exercise, but the cat was miserable in the very deep snow and we both tended to end up chilled to the bone. The New Year passed without incident, except that I began thinking of having some kind of celebration for the anniversary of Toby Jug's entry into my life.

The 21st of January loomed large in my mind with the memories of that fatal evening flooding back. I was now back at work and so I delayed any observance of the anniversary until the weekend after the exact date. On the Friday night I planned to give Toby a special birthday treat so I bought some sirloin steak for us both. The meal was a delight and I made a real fuss of him to show how much I loved him.

'You are a great cat and one of the best things that ever happened to me.' Luminous green eyes stared up at me full of affection and regard. 'Tomorrow,' I said, 'I will tell you the story of how you came to me, for your sake, and just to remind myself of how it all happened.'

On Saturdays I caught up with the many housekeeping chores that I didn't have time for during the week and, as the weather continued to be bleak, it was sensible to stay indoors so our country walks were put on hold. Towards evening I had finished most of my jobs and I decided to spend some time in the conservatory from which I was able to look out on the splendour of the garden and watch the birds feeding. I'd recently bought two oil-filled electric radiators to heat the room and so it was that I settled in there on a small settee with Toby Jug beside me.

I began to tell him the story of his life. I started with my memory of finding his mother, a beautiful, silver-furred she-cat, caught fast by a back leg in an iron trap. I heard her screaming with pain and frustration as I looked out from the conservatory door following a snow storm. I went out into the cold night and searched the area until I found her in the deep snow and managed to free her from the trap. Although she had been badly injured and had lost a lot of blood, once she was free she ran off despite her wounds.

Toby looked up at me from his position on my knee. His eyes were searching my face to gather the meaning of my words as I continued with the story, all the while stroking his head and back. He began to purr, which encouraged me.

I told him that I decided to try to find the injured cat again and see if I could help her because I have loved cats all my life. I followed her tracks through the snow and eventually found her on the top floor of an old barn.

I then realized why she had been in such a hurry to get away. 'It was because she was a mother and needed to return to care for her two tiny kittens, one of which was you and the other was your little brother,' I told Toby.

'I wrapped you all up in some sacking I found in the barn and took you to the vet's in Alnwick, but your mother and your brother could not be saved. I brought you back here to the cottage with me and, although you were very tiny, weak and sick, I managed to make you well so that you could live with me and be my friend. That, Toby Jug, is the story of your life and how you came to live here with me.' Toby tilted his head attentively. 'By the way, you got your name because I used to put you in a glass jug lined with cotton wool to keep you safe and warm when I was at work. It seemed only natural to call you Toby Jug. I had originally been toying with the idea of calling you Korky after the cat on the front of the *Dandy* comic, but Toby Jug suited you perfectly.'

When I finished the tale, I couldn't be sure whether any of it had registered meaningfully with my cat, but then my hopes were raised by what he did next, which astounded me. He rose up on two legs and, reaching over to my face, he gave my cheek several affectionate licks as sweet as a kiss. This was confirmation enough for me that somehow he had understood what I'd told him; at least, that was my hope. I added a postscript to the story for him by promising to take him, in the spring, on a pilgrimage to the barn where I had trailed his mother and found him, a tiny little ball of fur.

Strange to say, that night erupted with the worst storm in a decade. I awoke in the early hours to a drumming of hailstones against the windows and battering blasts of wind that swept through every crack and cranny in the ancient cottage. The draughts eerily whistled and whined their way around the rooms like ghosts and even ruffled my hair as I lay in bed.

Something else had also awakened me. Toby Jug was desperate to escape the freezing cold and seek warmth under the blankets alongside me. When I stroked him his fur felt cold and he was shivering, partly, I think, with fright. I was feeling the cold myself and in these harsh conditions drastic measures were needed so I retrieved two extra blankets from a cupboard and hunted out a thick pair of woollen socks to wear in bed. Only then did I begin to feel a tad more comfortable. Neither I nor Toby had ever heard such a gale before and I was worried that the roof might be badly damaged. The roaring of the wind seemed to go on for hours and it was only with the daylight that its force started to abate.

In the morning light, I went outside to see if there had been any damage to the cottage, but apart from fragments of broken tree branches littering the ground I was surprised to find that there were no other signs of devastation, thankfully, not even a loose roof tile. The wind was still blowing fiercely but with nothing comparable to the violence that had kept us awake most of the night. In the evening a snow storm blew in from the west and wild blizzards caused a complete whiteout. It seemed more than coincidence that such a storm, reminiscent of the tempest that had heralded the finding of Toby Jug in 1966, should arrive the night after I had told him the story.

THE PRIVATE LIFE OF TOBY JUG

Although the weather continued to be severe for the rest of January 1969 and all of February, the first few weeks of March brought with them a hint of spring. The first days of spring are always welcome after the severe, bitter Northumbrian winter. In the autumn I had planted some large earthenware containers with layers of bulbs, and the effort bore fruition with a whole series of different flowers appearing in turn in response to the extra sunshine. First came the delicate little snowdrops, followed closely by yellow and purple crocuses. Next the daffodils made their appearance, large King Alfreds jostling each other in the breeze to demonstrate their vivid yellow brightness as if they were determined to bring some golden cheer. Then came the massed red tulips, the aristocracy of the flower kingdom, to announce that spring had really arrived and summer wouldn't be far behind.

Toby Jug had an affection for flowers. Often in summer I'd see him in the garden rolling in the wild flowerbeds of cowslips, daisies and dandelions. Occasionally he would even smell the roses, but he steered well clear of any flowers with bees or wasps on them – possibly he'd been stung in the past and learned to avoid them. Since the weather was improving I was able to plant our small Christmas tree in the ground at the top of the garden, while attended by a curious cat. The tree had survived in the cottage over the holiday and then outside in its container pot. Now it had a chance to grow naturally in the soil at the top end of the garden.

I strolled down to the village several times a week, often to buy milk and bread from the shop which also housed the Post Office, a popular venue for locals to share the current gossip. Some distressing news I had picked up on one of my visits had me really worried. The rumour was that a gang of criminals was abducting cats and selling them to vivisection laboratories. Apparently there had been reports in the *Northumberland Gazette* and the *Newcastle Journal* of cats going missing, mainly in the Hexham area of Northumberland. It was therefore with mounting alarm that when I returned from work one evening in the first week of March Toby Jug could not be found.

I thought the worst. I searched everywhere to no avail. There wasn't a sign of him anywhere and I was worried sick. I pictured him going up to somebody in his friendly fashion and being abducted never to be seen again. I couldn't eat, I couldn't think straight. In total misery, all I could do was to tour the roads and alleyways in the village, hoping against hope that he hadn't been run over, trapped or shot by poachers or stolen. I uncovered two primed gin traps by the river bank and destroyed them in a fit of fury, but there was no sign of Toby. Weary to the bone, I returned to the cottage and brewed myself a mug of tea. I couldn't bear to think that he might have been taken for vivisection. How any so-called scientist can feel justified in tormenting and torturing a sentient animal is beyond my comprehension.

Plunged into despair at this thought, I was startled by a loud banging on the door. It was my neighbour Alice. She told me that she had been busy spring cleaning and had opened doors and windows to freshen the house. In the early afternoon she had gone into her bedroom and found a cat on her bed. She was afraid of cats so she immediately shut the door. Although she couldn't be sure it was my cat, she had been waiting for me to return home to get the cat out of her house.

With my heart beating wildly I raced around to her cottage and up the stairs to open her bedroom door. Sure enough, as soon as the door opened Toby Jug bolted out, dashed down the stairs and ran away. I apologized to Alice and returned to the cottage.

There was Toby, as large as life, sitting on the doorstep whining to be let in. I hugged and stroked him and I shed a tear or two in sheer relief I was so hyped up. The remainder of the evening was spent in joyous calm. As I fed the hungry cat I couldn't help once again recalling when Toby Jug had stolen tomatoes from Alice's greenhouse in the mistaken impression that they were red balls. Poor Alice! I'm not sure what she made of Toby Jug, but she would no doubt keep her doors closed from now on.

In view of the frightening tales of disappearing cats, I decided that Toby Jug should remain in the cottage after I left for work. I let him out in the garden whilst I had my morning cup of tea and toast overlooking the village towards the Cheviot Hills. Then I called him in where he could stay warm, sheltered and, above all, safe until I returned in the evening. I did this for some time until I began to feel more confident that our village was not a target for cat-abducting gangs.

On the next dry and sunny weekend I set out to fulfil my promise to Toby that I would retrace my steps to the place where he was born. Toby padded alongside me wearing his harness and lead as I traversed the tracks across fields and gorse-covered land that I had travelled on that challenging night. The journey was longer than I remembered and Toby Jug's energy began to flag just as we came in sight of the old barn, so I carried him the rest of the way.

The place was even more dilapidated than I recalled, but time had passed and I was now viewing it in bright sunlight. There was no sign of the ladder I had used, and the upper floor where the she-cat had given birth to her kittens looked as if it was in a state of collapse so I was afraid to venture further. I was able to show Toby some of the scratch marks on the wooden board that had been made by his mother on her way up to the top floor.

'This is it, Toby. This is where you were born and the place from which I rescued you. How about that?' I put him down and let him have a good sniff around but I couldn't be sure that the barn held any significance at all for him.

As we made our way home again I had to carry him, but back in the cottage he soon revived with a helping of some meat cuttings from a joint of silverside and I had a bowl of hot vegetable soup. I too felt fatigued by the day's efforts. I lay stretched out on the parlour floor in front of the fire as the April weather turned to rain and it became quite cold. Toby Jug curled himself up between the fire and my body, and in this sublime position of contented repose we both fell fast asleep.

My duties at Alnwick College sometimes meant that I spent long days at work leaving Toby Jug to fill time on his own, but I wasn't too worried now he was a grown-up cat of three and the stories of the cat abductions had faded away. Only gradually did I become aware of how he occupied himself whilst I was away. The first hint came from a neighbour who would sometimes make a passing remark in the newspaper shop and café, the Running Fox, at Felton.

'What a lovely, friendly little cat you have. He often comes to my windowsill and I save him treats of cheese and bacon.'

Soon I started to hear this sort of comment more often, sometimes from people I did not even know. In some village quarters, it seemed, Toby Jug was becoming extremely well known and liked. Most of his visits were to kind ladies in the cottages, but I was amazed one morning, later in that spring of 1969, to discover just how broad was his new circle of friends.

I was repainting the drive gates when a car suddenly pulled up and a vicar emerged to introduce himself as the minister from the United Reform Church further along the road.

'Hello!' he greeted me. 'You don't know me but I believe that I am acquainted with your cat who often visits my church some mornings whilst I am conducting a service and stays afterwards to share my lunch. He is such a jolly little fellow that I long to know his name and where he lives. Am I right in thinking he is your cat? Several of my parishioners speak of him only as that "dear little cat".'

Before giving him an answer I turned and whistled a signal for Toby Jug to come to me. He was busy foraging around at the top of the garden, probably chasing grasshoppers, and raced down in answer to my call.

'Is this the cat you mean?' I asked the beaming minister.

'It is indeed,' he said, with enthusiasm at the sight of Toby who was looking at me in a mystified way and obviously wondering why I had called him.

'His name is Toby Jug,' I said by way of introduction. By now the vicar was bending down to pat and stroke Toby, who responded with eager aplomb. We exchanged names and pleasantries before the Reverend David Martin drove off satisfied now that he knew the name of his only cat parishioner.

'So that's what you get up to when I'm away,' I said, but Toby simply trotted off back to his playtime concerns and I returned to my painting. It was no great surprise to me that Toby Jug occupied himself in a friendly manner when I was not there. After all, he was an extremely outgoing and amiable cat who was easily bored but inventive enough to arrange a stimulating agenda to fill his spare time. I applauded his ingenuity but felt slightly miffed that

I hadn't known about it. Nevertheless he had a right to a private life away from me, and I could not deny him that.

As far as him attending church services, I found this highly amusing. I considered it likely that Toby Jug's motives had more to do with socializing than religion, but who knows? After all, isn't God for everybody, humans and animals alike?

Soon other surprises came to light regarding the secret life of Toby Jug. A new family had moved into one of the cottages at the far end of the village. I hadn't met them, as I tended to keep to myself as much as possible, but one morning as I collected my newspaper from the Running Fox a stranger introduced herself as Elsie. She directed my attention to her puppy dog, a Bedlington terrier called Flopsy.

'She loves your cat,' she said. 'Whenever he appears on my windowsill she becomes terribly excited in a friendly way and I just have to let him in. They play together, having great fun chasing each other through the house, upstairs and downstairs at breakneck speed. Would you believe it?'

I stooped and fondled her puppy, a friendly little animal which, with her curly grey hair and floppy ears, looked just like a newborn lamb.

'I can believe it,' I replied. Toby Jug had previously befriended another dog, a miniature Yorkshire terrier, at a field study centre I was attending.

'Well, I hope you don't mind,' she said, 'but it's good for Flopsy to have a playmate and your cat shares my puppy's food bowl. Is that all right with you?'

'I don't mind at all,' I said. 'I'm glad to hear that Toby Jug has found a friend and I hope it lasts.'

'So his name is Toby Jug. I must remember that because I've just been calling him Pusscat.'

I laughed and nodded goodbye, but I wasn't sure that I wanted to share my cat with strangers. I drove away feeling somewhat piqued, but then I did leave him alone for long periods. He had obviously developed his own extensive contacts in the village and had become something of a celebrity cat. 'Well, good for him!' I muttered to myself.

Then one day I learned that his social calls didn't just extend to the church and village. For reasons best known to himself, he had trekked over half a mile from our cottage to visit Joe and Betty at Grove Farm. During a traumatic incident in his first year, Toby had been scared by the hounds of the Percy Fox Hunt and had taken refuge in a byre of the farm. There he had been befriended by a large male cat called Black Bob. I met Joe and Betty Green one Sunday morning at the Market on Amble quayside. They cheerfully told me that Toby Jug was in the habit of appearing occasionally at the farm and playing with Black Bob.

'Bob is a rough feral tomcat who wouldn't let another cat anywhere near him,' said Joe, 'but he's taken to your little Toby.'

At this point Betty took over the conversation. 'Well, I think we know why, don't we? It's because they're father and son. Animals know more than we ever give them credit for and we remember Bob courting the silver grey she-cat that was your cat's mother. You'll remember when you came to collect him that Bob lay with Toby Jug in front of the Aga after I'd washed him. They knew each other from the start, God only knows how.'

'The missus is always right!' said Joe, grinning apologetically.

This latest piece of news left me flabbergasted since I never dreamed that Toby Jug would travel that far, although he must have remembered how Betty had mothered him affectionately when the incident happened. As for Black Bob and Toby knowing each other, I had a sneaking suspicion that it might have been to do with scent, which in animals is often more important than appearances.

The news about Toby's visits to Grove Farm was intriguing to say the least and added a further dimension to my knowledge of his fascinating personality. One worrying factor about his wanderings was that his outgoing behaviour, especially towards strangers, rendered him vulnerable to attack since not everybody likes cats. Also wandering across the countryside could expose him to encounters with wild predators such as badgers, foxes and weasels, not to mention pine martens and large birds of prey. The dilemma for me was whether to restrict my cat to the cottage as a safety measure or take the risk of letting him run free to answer the call of the wild. Since ours is a small village peopled by friendly folk, I decided to leave things as they were and trust to fate, but I reserved the right to change my mind in the future if circumstances merited it.

I was soon to receive another shock about Toby Jug's private life.

I always left the top half of the gated door to one of the stone outhouses bordering the garden open. This was so that Toby Jug could take refuge inside if needs be when I was at college. There was a large cushion bed and a blanket laid across a shelf at his disposal, together with a water bowl in case he needed a drink. One Saturday when I came to clean the area, I was surprised to find a number of unusual items secreted under a corner of the blanket. There was a child's dirty mitten, several thick elastic bands of the type postmen discard from packs of letters, a small sponge, a matchbox, two horse chestnuts and, shock horror, a dead songbird, a greenfinch. He must have summarily collected this secret cache of objects for his own satisfaction. I had read that a distinctive feature of the Maine Coon breed was an ability to retrieve, but I was mystified by the covert aspects of his behaviour. I was beginning to realize that there were facets of Toby Jug's life that were a complete mystery to me.

I removed the bird corpse and left the rest. I decided that from time to time I would check the contents of this stash of collectibles but would not confront Toby. After all, it was his business. What fascinated me about the find was that Toby had deliberately concealed his collection, an act of wilful deception apparently for its own sake. It brought home to me the realization that it is possible to live with someone and yet not fully know them.

Yet dogs bury bones, foxes bury eggs, squirrels store nuts and mice dig up and hide flower bulbs in the garden. Human beings make all sorts of private collections as part of an urge to acquire things. Perhaps Toby was only expressing his normal instincts and doing what came naturally. Viewed in this light, Toby Jug's behaviour was perfectly understandable, but the items comprising his stockpile were still intriguing.

As regards temperament, Toby Jug, true to the recognized attributes of Maine Coons, was extremely affable and even-tempered, except when a rare circumstance arose which really displeased him. An example of this was his possessive domination of my footstool, which he commandeered for his own use exclusively. When I was sitting relaxing in the armchair by the fire I liked to have a footstool on which to rest my legs for added comfort, but Toby Jug did not like to share the stool with my feet so at times we vied with each other for custody. If he couldn't get on the stool because of my feet, he would get in a huff and start ripping at the carpet with his claws, which he was aware displeased me intensely. I would usually yell at him to stop scratching, but he would continue defiantly until I removed my feet.

I am fully aware that appeasing the aggressor only makes him more aggressive when he wants his own way, but I loved my cat and, for the sake of a peaceful relationship, I acquiesced most of the time when he employed this irritating tactic. He was just doing what a cat has to do, and it was part of his well-rounded personality.

It was a source of mild amusement to me that my normally easy-going friend had a feisty side to his character. This aspect of his temperament was evident when I made preparations for a working day trip in the car. I repeatedly had to lift him out of the car, where he would ensconce himself time and time again, to make it clear that on this occasion he couldn't come. When the moment for departure arrived Toby Jug could not be found. A thorough search of the cottage eventually detected his hiding place in the rear of a clothes cupboard where he was having a good old sulk. Lots of cuddles and strokes and several titbits of boiled ham turned around his bad mood and persuaded him that I still loved him and all would be well when I returned. At times, it was rather like living with a clinging and demanding child, but then it was probably my fault for indulging him so much.

TOBY JUG AND A HORSE CALLED LADY MAY

The place where I worked at Alnwick had many interesting aspects, and it was there, through contact with a colleague of mine, that I became acquainted with a horse that was to figure largely in my life – and that of Toby Jug. By the start of the summer term of 1969, Toby had become a proper little young adult cat. He had lost none of his kittenish charm, and he still wasn't very worldly-wise, but his skill in befriending both people and animals meant we were able to go on great adventures together.

Alnwick College of Education was housed in the medieval castle that was the seat of the Percy clan, the Dukes of Northumberland. The staff of the college comprised a small community of academics and support workers who, enfolded within the walls of the ancient fortress, tended to be a close-knit group. Everyone from the lecturers to the domestic staff knew each other by name. The austere surroundings imparted an awareness of the history of the site and I enjoyed the privilege of working in a building whose very rooms and corridors were linked to age-old traditions. For the most part it was a happy place in which the different departments cooperated with each other amicably for the benefits of the students, who were mostly young women with a small number of mature men, all training for the teaching profession.

On most days we gathered for a mid-morning coffee break in a large ancestral room overlooking what Gavin Maxwell, author of *Ring of Bright Water*, called 'the curtained walls' of stone enclosing areas of lawn. As I drank my coffee one morning, Jenny Howard, a lecturer in the Physical Education Department, sat next to me and mentioned that she was having great difficulty with one of the rescue horses she and her husband Barry had adopted. She'd heard that I had some experience with horses and riding and wondered if I could offer her any advice.

Since I believe that all animals are individuals, I explained that I would really need to meet the horse before I could offer any help. We arranged that I would come to her farm, which was somewhere in the Wooler Hills, on Saturday and I asked if I could bring my cat, Toby Jug, who had shown a liking for a horse in the past. She readily agreed but said that she would need to shut her large mastiff dogs away as they were unused to cats and quite ferocious. Barry had brought them to the farm chiefly to act as guard dogs.

On Saturday morning I did my shopping in Morpeth and, after a brief lunch, Toby Jug and I set off for Raven Crag Farm high in the hills above the Ingram Valley. The farm was situated in a small valley of its own with a stream running through it. I left Toby in the car while I was shown around. There were sheep and goats, some pigs, two donkeys and three horses. The donkeys and horses were animals rescued by the RSPCA charity. It seemed that Jenny and Barry were more interested in conservation than making a living as farmers, although they told me that their smallholding paid its way.

I was eventually introduced to the horses which, like the donkeys, had previously suffered brutality and abuse. They were free to roam in a large paddock with a long loosebox and plenty of fresh grass. The donkeys were docile creatures, which were inseparable, as were the two geldings, Roman and Bonny. However, the third horse, a grey mare known by the imposing name of Lady May, had proved most troublesome. She regarded me with a hostile gaze and snorted aggressively when I attempted to stroke her. Jenny said they were thinking of re-homing her because she had bitten Roman when he tried to make friends and she'd kicked out at Barry when he'd tried to saddle her. She had thrown a tantrum when they put her in one of the stables during a rainstorm and preferred to spend the day, when she wasn't grazing, brooding alone under the shade of a large chestnut tree at a far corner of the paddock.

Over a mug of coffee in the spacious kitchen, Jenny told me what she knew of Lady May's history. When the charity rescued her she'd been tied to a pole in a field with strands of barbed wire around her mouth and wound around her neck and body, which had torn her flesh and made her scream with rage as she tried to break free. A dirty carpet remnant had been draped over her, no doubt to cover her plight rather than as a comfort. Some hill walkers had heard her whimpering cries and alerted the police. In addition to being physically abused she'd also been starved and was described by those who found her as a bag of skin and bones. It seems that she had been abandoned by someone and just left to suffer and die. A torn manufacturer's label on the carpet contained the words 'Lady May St . . .' so she was named Lady May by her rescuers.

'We reckon she must be about eight years old and we despaired of ever rehabilitating her. We thought we'd give it a try and perhaps she'd recover her health in the company of the other two horses, especially with the provision of good feeding and loving attention.'

My heart sank as I absorbed this information. It was no wonder that Lady May had proved troublesome. Horses tend to be the gentlest creatures who respond with eager aptitude to training and human contact when accorded kindness and fair treatment, but mistreatment can cause deep psychological scars. I shook my head more in sorrow than anger and said I would like a little time on my own with Lady May.

I collected Toby Jug from the car together with a bag of young carrots and two apples from my garden store. We walked together along the outside of the paddock fence until we were opposite Lady May, who was standing beside the tree she favoured. I lifted Toby to the top of the fence and we all stared at each other. Using my routine method, I began talking to her.

'Hello horse, I've come to make friends with you and I've brought along my pal Toby Jug to meet you.'

Her ears pricked at the sound of my voice and she turned her head to look at us. I hoped the appearance of a little animal like Toby Jug wouldn't cause a nervous reaction. I have often found that the presence of another animal, be it a hen, a dog or a cat, can calm and reassure a fractious creature. I then extracted a thin carrot from the bag and began eating it. She soon picked up the scent of the carrot and turned full body to watch me. She gave me her full attention but didn't come closer. I spoke to her again.

'I have come to help you, horse. Be my friend.'

I dropped the remnants of the carrot on her side of the fence and carefully laid another carrot on top of a fence-post. Toby Jug was becoming bored and whined to me. On hearing him, Lady May whickered and shook her head up and down, which I took to be a good sign.

'We'll be back. Enjoy the carrot,' I said, and withdrew a fair distance to watch from behind a barn. After a short while the horse moved over to the ground beneath the fence and ate the stub of carrot I'd dropped there. Then, in a hasty movement, she took the carrot from the fencepost, retreated to her tree and munched it down.

'So far so good,' I said to myself. Meanwhile, Toby Jug had wandered inside the barn, much to the annoyance of a large red hen which clucked and flapped her short wings and tried to peck him. Toby sidled up to my legs and looked at me with a plaintive expression as if to say, 'What are we doing here? Can we go home?'

I picked him up and carried him back to the car. Jenny saw us and came over to find out what I thought. I told her not to expect miracles but that I would come back again the following weekend and do my best. I advised her to put the other horses and donkeys in a different field.

She nodded as I added, 'Lady May needs to feel secure. Leave her alone as far as possible and don't feed her any carrots or apples. Leave that to me and we'll see what happens. I like the horse and I'll try to befriend her if you'll permit me.'

She thanked me for coming and said she'd do what I asked.

I drove home thinking a lot about the horse. Lady May presented a challenge that I couldn't resist. Toby slept on the back seat all the way home. It seemed the trip had not been a pleasant one for him and had actually exhausted him. My strategy with Lady May would be the same as I used with all animals. That is, to persuade them to like me and to be my friend. All animals have feelings, and if I can make them feel good about being with me, then I can get close to them and train them. Lady May seemed to have nothing but bad feelings about herself because of the abuse she had suffered. I would try to change that for the better.

Meanwhile, word had got around via the village grapevine about where Toby Jug lived, and over the next week I had several callers enquiring where to obtain a kitten like him. I could only tell them that he came from Maine Coon stock and, as far as I knew, there were no more like him in the area. These queries reminded me what an exceptional cat I had, making me doubly anxious that someone might take advantage of his friendliness and steal him.

Over the next few weeks I continued to visit Lady May and take her carrots, which I had to leave either on the ground or the fence. Although she recognized me, she refused to come close and I spent my time simply familiarizing her with my presence and voice. On each visit I took Toby Jug along with me, but he wasn't all that happy at the farm. It might have been due to the random way in which the animals were allowed to roam about. Since my attention was mainly focused on the horse, I was only aware from a distance of what Toby Jug was up to. On one occasion two saddleback piglets had some fun chasing him, emitting screams and grunts. I thought they were just playing with him, but Toby became so scared that he clawed his way up a chicken coop and sat trembling on the roof. Not only was his dignity offended but he was terrified by the noise the piglets made and thought, I'm sure, that they meant to bite him and worse. The sight of him running in a panic from them no doubt presented a comical picture if it hadn't been so serious.

After the piglets moved away, Toby decided to seek refuge in the barn, only to be attacked by the rooster, which resented his closeness to the hens foraging about in there. I heard the aggressive shrieks of the cockerel and the hysterical clucking of the hens who believed they were being attacked by a predator. I rescued a much chastened cat, cowering in trepidation.

To his perceptions the farm was a place of fear and chaos, with dogs barking in their lock-up shed, pigs and a rooster running free. Poor cat, it just wasn't his day. Toby Jug was accustomed to an orderly life without threat in the cottage and village and was always relieved when it was time to leave the farm. On the next visit there he flatly refused to leave the car and spent the whole afternoon crouched miserably on the back window ledge, whining and pleading to go home whenever I looked his way.

I must admit that the way the farm was run bothered me, too. In relation to caring for animals, I think that they respond best to a well-organized and peaceful environment – anything to the contrary is unsettling. I suspected that Lady May could not adjust to the noise and undisciplined animal behaviour at Jenny's farm, which did nothing to quell her already nervous disposition. It was with relief that I soon learned of a new development which was to change matters for the better.

Jenny's father-in-law managed a country hostelry called the Fishing Boat Inn at Boulmer, close to the seashore. He also owned several adjacent fields, one of which had a stable and a loosebox and was bordered on the front side by a stone wall. One Monday morning during coffee break at the college, Jenny told me of her plan to move Lady May down to Boulmer at the weekend as a respite from the farm since she was not comfortable there. I volunteered to be there to meet the horse and help to settle her at the new site.

On Saturday afternoon, Toby Jug and I were in position awaiting Lady May's arrival. The horsebox carrying her duly arrived, driven by Barry, who admitted to not looking forward to handling the mare as she had bitten him twice. He was immensely relieved to find me waiting by the entrance to the paddock and I assured him that I would be happy to handle her on my own. Leaving Toby Jug to sit on the fence and watch the seagulls feeding on the beach, I slowly entered the trailer without touching the horse. She whinnied in alarm when she saw me because she didn't understand what was going to happen to her. I tried to calm her nerves by feeding her wedges of fresh apple and, for the first time, stroking her neck very gently. Wild-eyed nervousness gradually gave way to expressive snorts and her body began to lose its tension as my voice and strokes soothed her.

After half an hour, while holding her by the head band, I was able to back her out of the trailer and into the stable where I had laid out some chopped carrots, which she immediately started to eat. Whilst she chewed I softly spoke to her, explaining that she would be happier here with the sight and sound of the sea, which are very good for the relief of anybody's nervous disposition. At this stage of our relationship I decided not to stroke her too much – that would come later. She ostensibly relaxed and even turned her massive head to stare at me as if to say thank you.

There was only one interruption. It was Toby Jug. Tired of being left outside, he made his way into the stable and leapt onto the top of the wooden stall to the side of Lady May. Then he worked his way around until, balanced on the edge of the hay stall, he came face to face with the horse. Lady May was startled by his arrival but I was delighted to see both animals introducing themselves, nose to nose. Identities being duly identified through scent, both animals relaxed. Lady May gave a muted snort and a throaty snicker, and Toby Jug folded himself into a comfortable position opposite her.

It never fails to amaze me how separate species of animal are prepared to tolerate their differences and relate to each other in a friendly way. I have seen dogs become close companions of cats and I once heard of a racehorse that would not travel without the company of a red hen with which it had formed a bond. It reminded me of how Toby Jug had related to Fynn, a horse we rode on a trip into the Cheviot Hills during Toby's first year. If, as it seemed, Lady May took to Toby Jug, it would certainly smooth the path as I attempted to train her.

I heard voices outside, and on leaving the stable was introduced to Barry's father, Jack Whitlock. I was informed that when Jenny wasn't there, the horse would be well cared for by the family, especially his two teen-age daughters who were ecstatic at the prospect of having a horse on the premises. For my part I could see nothing wrong with Lady May having some extra love and adulation, which was just what she needed in abundance to make her feel right about herself and the universe in general. I was greatly reassured – although the family made it clear that I was welcome whenever I liked, I wouldn't be able to visit every day. I explained that I hoped to train Lady May to the saddle and ride her in the future, and that my cat and I already felt an attachment to her.

It was a bright gusty day and huge waves pounded the shore, making an exhilarating sight. This was my kind of country and I was sure it would prove better than the farm for the rehabilitation of Lady May. After Barry left to drive back to the farm, I bought a cool lager from the bar to drink outside in sight of the sea. Lady May, who was not tethered, eventually came out of the stable and explored her new paddock. After a couple of circuits she stopped to graze near the fence where I sat with Toby Jug. It seemed as if things were going to turn out all right.

I felt an easy contentment with life, lounging close to a beach on a sunny afternoon in May, watching a horse and stroking a cat. After finishing my drink, I stretched out on the grass amidst the cowslips and buttercups and dozed the afternoon away, lulled by the soothing swish of the sea which grew calm as evening approached. I must have fallen asleep, and when I awoke Toby Jug was lying across my chest and I could hear Lady May cropping the grass nearby. As I arose and stretched my stiffened limbs, Toby Jug commenced giving himself a tongue-wash but became anxiously alert when several long-winged seagulls alighted near us looking for scraps of food. I returned my empty glass to the bar and made my farewells with the promise of another visit soon.

I drove home on narrow, winding and delightfully empty country roads bordered by thick hedges and trees in full summer bloom. The scent of honeysuckle and wild roses wafted through my partly open window, while overhead the trees formed a green canopy allowing only an occasional streak of light to form dappled patterns on the road. I revelled in the warmth of this early summer day in May that seemed to make my self-appointed task of training Lady May a lot easier. When Toby and I arrived back at the cottage it was late and the last of the sunlight was giving way to dusk.

I spent Sunday in the greenhouse pruning and feeding tomato and cucumber plants which were responding well to the increasing light and heat as summer began to approach. Toby Jug had found an empty cardboard box on the potting bench to cuddle into. He paid rapt attention as I conversed with him during my ministrations with the plants. Ever heedful of my words, his green eyes sparkled as I explained the miracle of nature in which a tiny seed, no bigger than a crumb, planted in fertile soil could grow into a large flowering plant bearing delicious fruits. As the time passed I introduced him to Einstein's equation $E=MC^2$, and explained some of the mysteries of the universe which affected all of our lives, man and cat. As I talked to him I could feel the bond between us growing stronger. I knew that my Toby Jug gained in self-esteem through the intimate way I related to him, person to cat, even if he was unlikely to grasp all the physics.

As the weeks rolled by I spent many hours talking to Lady May and leading her round the paddock. I groomed her regularly in the stable, which was kept in good order by the efforts of Susan and Maureen, the teenage daughters of Jack, the owner of the Fishing Boat Inn. Towards the end of June I decided it was time to introduce her to the saddle. Toby Jug, as usual, accompanied me on my visits and I could tell that he did his best to help me befriend the horse, who appeared to have developed a real liking for him and whinnied a greeting when she saw him.

I led her outside to the fence and tethered her from the

headband. Then I fed her several wedges of apple from the store I had kept from last year's orchard yield and I finally slipped the iron bit into her mouth with ease as I draped the reins attached to the harness over her head. Then I placed a blanket over her back, all the while making encouraging comments like, 'There, now. Doesn't that feel okay? Good horse, good horse.'

At last I placed the saddle over the blanket, but as I tightened the cinch she half-raised a back leg as if to kick me. Her body tensed and went rigid but gradually relaxed as I soothed her with strokes and endearments. Then, undoing the tether, I led Lady May around the paddock many times, sometimes breaking into a trot as we ran side by side and I began to get the feeling that she trusted me. Toby Jug watched from a safe distance and mewed each time we passed. I guessed he wanted to be involved, so eventually I placed him on the saddle and brought Lady May around for a few more circuits at a gentle walk. Lady May turned her head when we stopped and looked at Toby on her back as if to say: 'That's all right with me, you're welcome to ride on my back.'

I was delighted with the progress and unsaddled and removed her harness. I slapped her on the rump and she frisked away around the field, tossing her head and whinnying. I sat on the grass with Toby Jug as we watched her delight at simply being a horse with the freedom to run as she pleased. As Lady May romped across the paddock the wind from the sea caught her mane and it billowed like white silk. After a while she came to us as if to give thanks, nuzzled my face and bent to Toby Jug who rose on his back legs to meet her nose to nose. This represented extraordinary progress. I had achieved a major goal and soon I would ride her.

Before I left, I encouraged the two girls to continue the good work of keeping a caring eye on her. I knew that Jenny and Barry also regularly came to stock up the stable with hay and grain and to check on her progress. One of our visits coincided and Jenny assured me that she was much relieved at my intervention and satisfied to leave the rehabilitation and training of Lady May entirely to me.

Back at the cottage there was much to be done in the garden. The fruit trees were coming into blossom – plum first, followed by pear and finally apple. The hazel tree seemed to have its own agenda, which I couldn't fathom. I never got any nuts from it because a family of red squirrels from the nearby pine woods gathered the harvest each year and I was pleased to have it so. The luxuriant blossom of the fruit trees attracted minor swarms of bees and greenfinches and yellowhammers. Songbirds, especially thrushes and blackbirds, stole some buds before they could open, but I wasn't bothered. In my garden wildlife had the first option on any fruit, berries and buds that grew there.

At college there was also plenty of work. Marking essays and assignments and teaching-practice supervision of students meant a lot of time-consuming travel. I was often able to take Toby Jug with me and he proved good company on long journeys up to places like Lauder, Duns and St Abbs in the Scottish Borders. Toby Jug loved accompanying me on these visits and never gave even a hint of trouble. We got along just fine as long as I made sure that I put his harness on and gave him a short walk in some of the wild places on our way, which were only inhabited by grouse, woodcock and long-haired, rust-coloured highland cattle with huge horns, which belied their amiable nature. I carried the requisite supply of water, dry biscuits and snacks for him as well as a packed lunch and flask for myself. Once, in Eyemouth, I bought some freshly cooked rolled herring, which was a refreshing and appetizing change for both of us from the picnic food I normally carried.

In the car Toby Jug proved an accomplished traveller. He adopted a variety of positions on our journeys. Sometimes he would rest on the passenger seat of my white Mini; at other times he preferred to lie on the rear shelf where he appeared to enjoy sliding about as I rounded corners. While on the shelf, he would cause much excitement in other cars, especially amongst child passengers who would wave and laugh as they passed us. At times he slept snug on the rug on the back seat, but one of his favourite positions was balanced on my left shoulder, purring in my ear but always maintaining the sangfroid expression of the experienced traveller as he gazed directly ahead. Nothing daunted him even if I suddenly had to brake; he would just lean forward and resolutely dig in his claws, which did neither the skin of my shoulder nor the fabric of my coat any good at all. It was fortunate that I had been able to accustom Toby to travelling in the car from an early age. He exalted in it, whereas most cats do not like travelling in vehicles at all.

The next time I was free to call on Lady May was the bank holiday weekend at the very end of May. Since the roads were crammed with long lines of cars and caravans I was happy not to travel far afield but simply to enjoy the quiet of a summer's day by the sea, tending a horse. Lady May seemed pleased to see us because, as usual, I was accompanied by Toby Jug. When we arrived, she would often be browsing in the shade of a horse chestnut tree at a secluded corner of the paddock. On catching sight of us she would whinny excitedly and gallop towards us in welcome. I deliberately spent long moments stroking her neck and flanks and telling her how beautiful she was and how much we loved her. I sometimes brought with me a bowl of linseed mash, which I made up for her back at the cottage. She relished these gifts of a special feed, and the show of affection, and they bound us even closer. Someone had brutalized this horse and ruined her self esteem. I saw it as my job to give her back her trust in human beings. Lady May responded to the unconditional love Toby Jug and I extended to her and had become a different horse from the one I first met. She was ready to ride and we could share some happiness in the process.

This time I'd brought her some young sweet carrots, which I knew would give her pleasure, and while she was eating I slipped on her bridle and bit. Then I saddled her and tightened the cinch across her belly. She didn't even make a pretence of kicking. Finally came the moment of truth when I stepped into the stirrup and swung slowly onto her back.

She neither protested nor demured as I sat rock steady,

careful not to make a sudden movement that might unnerve her. After a short wait she shifted her legs to achieve a better balance and so I tightened the reins and ever so gently nudged her forward with my knees. To my immense relief she paraded like a show horse around the paddock.

Acting on impulse and taking a chance at this early stage, I manoeuvred her near the gate and we walked at a steady pace out towards the beach. I pressed her flanks with my knees slightly more firmly this time and, to my delight, she broke into a trot. I had often tried to fathom how such a beautiful horse had been so mismanaged. She had obviously been ridden at some time in her life as I could feel her responding to my knees and gentle pressure on the reins.

Riding along the seashore with the wind in my face brought back fond memories of times past and I quite forgot about Toby Jug. Looking back over my shoulder, I spotted his forlorn, dark little figure sitting upright on the fence, and although I could not hear him from that distance I knew that he would be wailing. Well, first things first. There would be time enough to placate Toby Jug later, but for now I concentrated on the horse and urged her towards the edge of the sea. She responded with gusto and pranced through the wavelets, seeming to enjoy the salty tang of the sea in her nostrils and the cool water on her legs. As I turned her back towards the paddock she eased into a joyous cantor.

'What a wonderful horse you are!' I called to her above the sound of the waves. On that day happiness was a horse called Lady May.

I rode out with her every day of that holiday weekend. It felt as if I had been riding her all my life – the experience was so fulfilling that when we were out riding it felt like rider and horse became as one. I was so fond of her that I hated to miss a single day and not see her, but during term time my work at the college kept me so busy that almost a week would pass before I could visit again.

Meanwhile, there was the problem of what to do with Toby Jug when I went riding. During our adventures with Fynn when Toby was very young, I had used panniers to transport him, but they now seemed unsuitable as Toby was a mite bigger and I doubted whether Lady May would tolerate them on her back. I still had my large saddle bags, but I did not think that Toby would be comfortable jammed into one of them and tied behind me on the saddle.

Eventually I hit on the idea of a baby-carrier, which I had seen used by couples with very young children. It consisted of a supported miniature sleeping bag, slung around the neck of the adult or strapped onto the parent's back, in which the baby could lie comfortable and secure. The alternative was to leave Toby at home and I did not feel I could do that, but it all depended on whether he would accommodate being transported in this unusual way. During the following week I paid a visit to the baby shop in Alnwick town centre and bought a baby carrier. When I examined it I was reminded of Native American tribeswomen carrying babies in a papoose.

Affable and docile Toby Jug allowed me without objection to fit him inside the baby carrier. He looked somewhat bemused as to what was happening but accepted that if I was doing it then it would be all right. In fact, he appeared to enjoy being in the bag as it was lined with a warm, woolly fabric. The deciding sign of approval was when he snuggled into the carrier and began to purr. Satisfied with this arrangement, I put the carrier on my back, with Toby still inside, and walked around the cottage. I ventured out into the garden to see how he would take it. He made no fuss at all and at one point raised his head above the rim of the bag and happily looked around. It would have seemed comical to anyone watching, but I was more than satisfied. Toby Jug could now come riding with me in his new papoose just like a little Apache brave.

All of these developments started me thinking again about camping and I formed an idea to take Lady May on a camping trek along the coast. A possibility, I thought, would be to make a camp near Dunstanburgh Castle, which lies on a headland along the coast between the villages of Craster and Embleton. First of all, I would need to check out my plan with Jenny and Barry, but if they had no objection then I reckoned I could venture forth in late July or early August, weather permitting.

Jenny and Barry were all for it and surmised that it would be a real treat for Lady May. They even volunteered to provide back-up support if necessary.

Once I had fixed my mind on carrying out the expedition, I grew increasingly excited at the prospect of actually seeing it through. I didn't explain it to either Toby Jug or Lady May but I was sure they would be all for it. I have always found it uplifting during the everyday work routine to have something special to which to look forward, and so it proved in this instance.

I greatly enjoyed the exercise of making all the preparations needed to ensure the trip would go well. Over the following weeks, I took time out whenever I could to research the history of Dunstanburgh Castle. Built in 1313 by Thomas, Earl of Lancaster, it was badly damaged in the fifteenth century during the Wars of the Roses and has remained a ruin ever since. Most interestingly, it is believed that the castle is haunted. The earl led a failed rebellion against King Edward II and was executed for high treason. His beheading was particularly gory – the inexperienced executioner had to strike eleven blows with the axe before his head was severed from his body. Sightings of the earl's ghost carrying his mutilated head have been reported by walkers near the ruins. Other ghosts seen there are a knight, Sir Guy the Seeker, and a 'White Lady' who threw herself onto the rocks below the East Tower on learning of the death of the earl. Her wraith-like appearance has often been witnessed by fishermen travelling along that stretch of the coast at night. The tongue-in-cheek gossip around Craster is that these ghostly apparitions impart a wicked curse on any who see them. I intended to make my camp in the shelter of the castle ruins, ghost or no ghost, but I would keep a wary eye out.

Pending the camping expedition, one of the immediate priorities was to make sure that Lady May had the stamina for the coastal trek. At times we would need to travel by road and it was this factor which concerned me since

I wasn't sure whether the horse could cope with riding alongside road traffic. On warm summer evenings, especially at the weekends, I took Lady May on road training exercises. At first, I needed a firm hand and a soothing voice to quell her nerves at approaching cars and in particular at bad-mannered drivers who came up fast behind us and impatiently tooted their car horns. By and by, Lady May responded well to the schooling. One of the factors that I believed helped the horse to cope with the stress of road traffic was the fact that I sang to her as we rode along. Whilst I do not have an especially good voice, I think it was the calming sound of my singing which assured her that all was well.

I also took Lady May on short trips along the sandy beaches. Toby Jug, secure in the papoose strapped on my back, shared the road and the beach excursions, and jolly delighted he was too. I would ride along a beach until I reached a place all to ourselves. Then, as a matter of course but also to accustom the horse to campfires and camping procedures, I would light a fire in the sand from dry seaweed and driftwood and bake sausages on flat stones around the fire. I would unsaddle Lady May, knowing by now that she wouldn't desert me, and let her graze on the dunes and sometimes play in the sea. Toby Jug would lie in the sand to watch proceedings, especially the cooking sausages.

Once we stayed around the beach and the sand dunes extra late before returning to the paddock, as we were lured to dwell longer by the beauty of the wild landscape and seduced by the moonlight on the sea. We cantered along the water's edge to the accompaniment of crashing waves while sea spray dampened our faces. An unrestrained 'Hurrah' escaped my lips and at the sound Lady May flattened her ears, stretched her neck and galloped ahead like a racehorse, her hooves digging deep imprints in the wet sand and sending the blood pounding in my ears. At my back I heard a distinct 'Mew' from Toby Jug, secure in his papoose. He was simply echoing my own high spirits, such is the rapport between soulmates. For a brief moment horse, man and cat were united in the reality of feeling supremely alive. I urged my mount on with abandon, wishing it would all never end. It was a night never to be forgotten.

My plan for the camping trip was simplicity itself. I intended chiefly to follow the coastal paths from the paddock at Boulmer along to Dunstanburgh. I had already visited the Sugar Sands near Howick with Lady May, which was just a short jaunt along the coast, and decided to camp somewhere on that stretch the first night. There was a path leading down from the village of Longhoughton to a headland overlooking the sea. I had driven there many times in the past and parked above the small, sheltered sandy bay. A freshwater stream ran down from Howick Hall and where it made its exit to the sea there was an ideal campsite strewn with driftwood, which would prove very handy. Three miles further on would lead us to Craster village, which we could bypass over the crags, and then veer down to the path along the coastal stretch to the castle, where I would camp nearby. An arrangement was made for Barry to meet us with the horsebox at the beach end of the road from Embleton when the trip was over.

I still resolved to mount the camping trip later in the summer when warm weather was most likely. Planning so far in advance added to the happy anticipation of having a mini-holiday in the company of Toby Jug and Lady May, of whom I had become increasingly fond. Meanwhile, I was extremely busy at college in May and June, with third-year students out on their final teaching practice in rural schools before the final academic exams. This meant lots of supervisory visits to schools and a great deal of exam marking. Normally weekends were free, but providing additional tutorials for struggling students put further demands on my time.

On one especially fine summer morning I had arranged to visit schools in the Seahouses, Bamburgh and Beadnell areas. I decided to take Toby Jug with me and spend the whole day there to take advantage of what is a most picturesque part of Northumberland. It turned out to be an excellent day workwise, with all the students doing well and no problems to worry about. As I finished my supervisory duties by early afternoon I decided to take time out and spend an hour or two having a late picnic lunch on Bamburgh beach in full sight of the magnificent medieval castle. I called at Carter's, the butcher's shop in Bamburgh, and bought a hot pork-belly sandwich with crackling for me and a thin slice of cooked beef for Toby Jug. We had an idyllic late afternoon and evening, watching the fading sunlight on the seascape.

It wasn't until the lengthening shadow of Bamburgh Castle reached us that I reluctantly made a move to return to the car. As I drove along the beach road towards

Beadnell, I could see boats on the horizon taking advantage of a relatively calm sea, and the bright sunset picked out in sharp relief the Farne Islands, which appeared in the refracting light to be a mere stone's throw away.

Toby Jug sat comfortably on my shoulder as I drove, and I was aware of his little head whizzing from side to side as he also seemed to be admiring the attractive scenarios around us. It had been a splendid day when the normally harsh Northumbrian landscape had softened as a relief from grey skies and rough seas.

As each day passed I began to think with sharper focus about preparations for the camping trip. I needed to estimate the amount of food to take for me, Toby and Lady May. There was a limit to how much the saddle bags could hold and I had to take into account that I would already have a backpack in the form of the papoose to accommodate Toby Jug. The tent, blanket, sleeping bag and the bare minimum of cooking utensils (a frying pan, pot, mug and two small dishes) would have to be tied behind the saddle if the horse permitted, a tactic which had yet to be tried and tested. As well as dried milk powder I would also need room for a bottle of water and, as a luxury item, a bottle of Chablis together with a wine glass. A hip flask, holding brandy for emergencies, would fit in my jacket. Then there was the question of what to wear. The night temperatures on the north-east coast can vary a great deal, but it was wiser to predict colder weather than warm at night. I had a sheepskin jacket but I also needed a thick sweater.

With this in mind I paid a visit to the wool shop situated in The Shambles, a cloistered, stone-flagged pathway beneath the old town hall in Alnwick. The lady in charge was very helpful and obliged me by ordering a knitted chunky sweater in russet red, which she assured me would be ready in three weeks' time. Nine balls of the requisite wool were ordered and despatched to the knitter. That, I thought, should keep me warm no matter how inclement the weather.

At the first opportunity, I harnessed and saddled Lady May and, as a trial run, loaded her up with the items I meant her to carry on the trip. Jack's two girls watched in fascination as I positioned everything on Lady May's back as neatly as I could to allow for her comfort. Then I fed her wedges of eating apple as I led her slowly around the paddock perimeter several times. So far so good – Lady May showed no objection or even irritation.

'What a good horse you are!' I said, stroking and patting her neck and flanks. Next came the moment of truth as I made to mount up. The girls were highly amused when I slid Toby Jug into the papoose carrier and hoisted it onto my back. Gently sticking my foot in the stirrup, I climbed aboard her back and sat immobile for a minute or two. There was no reaction from Lady May except for a slight shuffling of her feet to adjust the weight. This was better than expected and I carefully nudged her forward. The girls laughingly applauded us as I left the paddock and rode Lady May along the beach.

The ride went like a dream, and when I had returned to the paddock and unpacked Lady May, I felt a blessed relief that all had gone according to plan. I set Toby free and then I fed, watered and groomed the horse and later repaired to the bar of the Fishing Boat Inn for a large glass of red wine and a bag of my favourite crisps.

'Job well done,' I concluded, much satisfied.

The camping trip was all set to go. I would repeat this afternoon's exercise several times to make sure that all would go well on the trip. Lady May, bless her heart, had proved herself an all-round gem of a horse and I was delighted with her performance, but I knew she had variable moods and could, on occasion, prove obstinate. I was banking on the assumption that her trust in me would carry us through any problems that might arise.

In the meantime there was some spring cleaning and gardening to do back at the cottage. Toby Jug hated the sound of the vacuum cleaner and would slope off somewhere in the cottage to hide away from the noise. One day when I was sorting through my clothes after having given the whole cottage a good carpet clean, I happened across his secret hiding place. Somehow he had managed to prise open the wardrobe door and secrete himself in a corner. When I opened the door to his concealed spot he emerged looking slightly ruffled and probably miffed at having been discovered. He stalked off with his tail upright as if to reprimand me for creating noise and upset in what was usually a domain of tranquillity.

Worse was to come. Toby Jug, having retreated to the peace of the garden and found a restful patch of dandelions and buttercups in which to lie, was to be again rudely disrupted by the thunderous approach of the petrol-powered lawnmower cutting the grass. I caught a brief glimpse of a cat in full flight as he streaked away to find sanctuary elsewhere. I couldn't help chuckling to myself at his evident indignation, because in so many ways Toby Jug led a charmed life with me as the servant attendant to his every need.

Sure enough, he was right on time for his dinner at six o'clock and he appeared as affable as ever, a true expression of his Maine Coon breeding. I gave him lots of strokes to soothe him and gave him an extensive spruce-up with a special brush I kept for the purpose. This made him relax and purr with sheer delight at having his fur thoroughly groomed. I decided then that on the next hot day when I was not at college, I would give him a midsummer bath to keep him clean of mites and fleas, a routine in which he exulted since he loved a warm bath.

On the next occasion that I visited Lady May it was one of those delightful mornings when the surface of the sea was as calm as a mill pond because there was no wind. The sheer beauty of it made me want to be on the camping trip and close to nature even more. All saddled up with Toby tucked into his papoose on my back, I set off on impulse to ride the coastal path to Alnmouth.

Lady May was in excellent form as she frisked along at a steady, mile-eating trot. She was proving to be a magnificent mount and it was a joy to ride her with the cool fresh sea air in my face and the winsome charm of the English countryside embracing us with a new view at every turn of the path. When we reached the beach area the tide was out and the smooth sands stretched out flat and inviting before us. I could feel Lady May's body throb between my knees as she gathered herself for an all-out gallop. I leant forward, loosened the grip on the reins and let her have her head.

The ride was a sublime experience as we raced along the open foreshore with the sea on one side of us and the undulating green patches and grassy knolls of a golf course on the other. I reined her back as we drew near to the mouth of the River Aln and several barking dogs circled us, exuberant with the chase. Unfazed, Lady May plodged in the frothy wavelets lapping the foreshore. She was having the time of her life and I was glad to share it with her.

As the tide began to turn I guided her along a track, overgrown with long stalks of sea aster, giant hogsweed and wavering dune grasses, to the road through sleepy Alnmouth, quiet even for a Sunday morning. We rode the high road on our way back to Boulmer, passing the vista of the immense oxbow bends in the river below us. We swung right at the crossroads leading down to Lesbury village and headed east under the bridge with Boulmer beach already coming into sight.

During the whole ride, I don't think Toby Jug ever raised his head. True to his cat nature, I expect he had enjoyed a comfortable snooze induced by the rhythmic motion of his papoose as we jogged along.

I led Lady May straight to the stable, and fed and watered her once she had cooled down. She had raised quite a sweat on the ride and the exercise had done her good. She seemed in fine spirits and whinnied farewell when I left her. I bought an ice cream from a van parked by the beach to cool me down. I then left Toby Jug in the stable with the horse as I made my way into the bar for a cool beer. It had been an excellent morning for everyone concerned and it was now time to relax in what remained of the summer day.

Preparations for the camping trip were now well in hand and there were just a few matters to conclude at college before the break. Final exam marks needed to be ratified by external examiners and pass lists posted to be scanned by anxious students. It was a great relief to round off another academic year and to be able to think of holiday times ahead. I was in the second year of my part-time study for a Master of Education degree at Newcastle University and I still had to finish my thesis, which was weighing heavily on my mind. Nevertheless, it was a respite to finalize arrangements with Barry and Jenny to meet me on the sliproad above Embleton Bay after three days' camping. All seemed to be going well, and five days after the college closed for the vacation I was ready for the journey ahead.

A CAMPING ADVENTURE AND A
SAD LOSS

E arly on a sunny morning in mid-July I set off by car from the cottage with Toby Jug balanced on my shoulder to rendezvous with Lady May in the paddock at Boulmer Sands. As soon as she saw me she trotted from her customary place under the chestnut tree to greet us. She was in fine fettle, as Jenny had remarked to me in college one morning.

'I can hardly believe the change in her,' she said. 'You've done wonders with that horse. She was a total wreck when we got her.'

I was glad to hear these comments because a disturbing incident had come to my attention concerning Lady May. Apparently during the half-term school break Susan and Maureen, the aforementioned daughters of the proprietor of the Fishing Boat Inn, had decided to have a ride on Lady May. They had got as far as placing the saddle on her back, but when they tried to tighten the conch Lady May realized what was happening and threw a tantrum, kicking and screaming until the blanket and saddle slipped off her back. Neither of the girls was hurt but this episode had shocked and frightened them.

When I heard about what had happened I sought to explain that Lady May was a nervous horse and had only just learned to trust me. She needed to feel secure and safe with whoever handled her and it had taken me a long while to convince her that I meant no harm. The magic ingredient in relating to animals, I explained to the girls, is tender loving care. It's the same as with people. The girls were normally very loving and caring with Lady May, but they must have frightened her by attempting to saddle her without me being there. I promised to try and familiarize the horse with them in the future, possibly by letting them have a go at riding double with me.

After hearing about this escapade I was worried that Lady May's trepidation would transfer to her relationship with me. Her prevailing temperament was crucial to the success of the camping trip, but I need not have worried. She responded to me and Toby Jug as usual and seemed as eager as ever to greet us and partake of the usual offering of sweet carrots and apples. Reassured, I set about loading her for the trip with the tent, the sleeping bag and the heavy saddle bags containing the essential supplies. Lastly I hung a canteen of water from the front of the saddle and, with Toby Jug secure in his papoose, we set off.

Thankfully there were no spectators except the usual flocks of seabirds, chiefly black-headed gulls and kitti-wakes swooping and diving along the shore. The schools had not yet broken up for the summer recess and so even the two girls, who were anxious to make amends to Lady May, were not in attendance. I checked my watch, which read 9.47 a.m., and the adventure, for better or worse, had begun.

We headed north out of Boulmer Haven at a fast trot blown along by a fresh breeze from the sea at our backs to encourage us on. It seemed in no time at all that we sighted the headland above the Sugar Sands as we moved onwards to the breakwater where a stream met the sea at Howick Sands. The sun was well up in the sky by now and the day promised to be a hot one. We were all alone except for two small fishing boats tossing around a few hundred yards out to sea.

I decided there and then to make an early camp. I dismounted and unpacked Lady May and then led her a short distance upstream where fresh green grass grew in abundance. Here I hobbled her and left her to graze. Nearby a small escarpment above the beach offered an ideal spot to pitch the tent and store the saddle and other baggage. Then I busied myself collecting driftwood for the huge fire I intended to light. There is nothing to beat a campfire for company, not to mention its uses for cooking and to provide warmth during what could be a cold night.

When everything was in order I took time out to indulge in a spell of beachcombing, something I love doing. It doesn't matter to me if I don't come across an interesting find, although that is always a possibility. It is more the simple pleasure of walking freely without a specific purpose in mind, to just enjoy being part of the colourful wonder of the great big sky and the roar of the sea, preferably barefooted to relish the memory of childhood days playing in the sand. In reality, it is a fine excuse for doing nothing and wasting time, but why not now and again to keep the spirit healthy? The closer a person gets to nature in the wild, the more the cares and woes of everyday life tend to slip away.

My erstwhile friend and invaluable companion in all of this was, of course, Toby Jug, on whom I depended to provide a balanced reality check on my life. To watch my cat scampering along the shoreline, stopping now and then to investigate a clump of seaweed or to charge feeding seagulls and send them wheeling and screaming in indignation, served only to garnish my delight that afternoon.

Suddenly I was jerked back to my responsibilities by the sounds of a horse whinnying and calling. In many respects horses behave like big dogs in that they hate being left alone. Lady May, after feeding her fill, had begun to feel lonely and, being in a strange place, had decided to summon us back. I stroked and soothed her, saddled up and took her for a short ride along the beach to atone for my neglect. Toby Jug was content simply to follow us at his own pace. Lady May insisted on stopping occasionally, which flummoxed me until I realized that she was looking back to check where Toby Jug might be. It struck me then that when animals form a bond they watch out for each other. I have long ceased to be mystified at animal behaviour, which I find is just as firmly based on emotions as it is with humans, but they are rarely given credit for this. 'Now we really are a threesome,' I thought to myself as I sang the opening bars of the Rodgers and Hammerstein song 'Oh, What a Beautiful Mornin' '. Lady May pricked her ears but did not otherwise react to my singing as we rode along.

Later we all settled down for a restful evening by our campsite. Lady May had been fed some grain to keep up her stamina and water to quench her thirst, and was now hobbled on a bankside in plain sight of us. I also tethered her on a long rope that I secured by wrapping it around a heavy stone. I didn't think that she would wander off, but it gave me peace of mind to know that she could not.

Toby Jug was lounging by the fire, stretched out to take maximum benefit from the heat and yet keeping a hungry eye on the rashers of bacon sizzling in the pan alongside my tin of beans. I was relaxing too, sitting with my back against a boulder with a glass of Chablis conveniently to hand. The pale dry white wine from Burgundy was a delightfully soothing complement to the summer evening. As the salt-soaked driftwood sparked and spluttered, sending a miniature storm of fiery flares into the darkening air, I was revelling in the thrill of being outdoors and feeling the freedom, as Thomas Gray put it, 'Far from the madding crowd's ignoble strife'. As Toby Jug and I stretched out together by the fire, I was enchanted by the starlit sky and the sound of the surf a few yards from us. I found myself already responding to the liberating aura of the trip. The cat, the horse and I were alone in a delightfully restful place. We would all sleep well tonight.

Waking up in a tent is rarely a cosy experience. For instance, the temperature tends to be below the level of warmth that invites activity so the tendency is to make you want to snuggle down deeper into your sleeping bag and review the situation. I awoke early. It was barely five o'clock and it felt cold. The orange fabric of my tent was alive with colour from the morning sun and I could hear the pounding of waves against the shore immediately outside.

I looked around and registered the unspecified note of alarm that had been nagging away at me. Toby Jug was nowhere to be seen. I recalled him lying close to my chest on the outside of the sleeping bag when I settled down for the night. Now he was gone, but where?

I could hesitate no longer and made the effort to get up and stagger outside. I whistled and called, shielding my eyes from the glare of the sun on the sea, but could not see him anywhere. Meanwhile, Lady May began whinnying and neighing for attention and I felt duty-bound to stroke and pat her, and dig out some grain and horse nuts to satisfy her hunger for breakfast.

Still no sign of Toby. Then my sleep-fogged brain commenced to work and I had an idea. Often, on cold mornings at the cottage when I had to make an early start to the day, I would discover that my cat had sneaked into bed during the night and found a snug berth deep down under the blankets.

Returning to the tent, I felt along the length of the sleeping bag and, sure enough, there was a suspicious lump right near the bottom. I thrust my hand right inside and the lump stirred into life as a warm furry ball of cat known as Toby Jug.

My relief was mixed with laughter at his prowess in always looking after number one. He emerged quite unconcerned, blinking in the harsh light and eager for breakfast as I could tell from the feverish way he commenced to freshen himself with a tongue-wash.

After unhobbling Lady May and leading her upstream to drink her fill, I delved into the saddle bag to retrieve a potato wrapped in cooking foil and placed it on a flat stone near the fire, which I had already revived. Next I opened a small tin of wild Alaskan salmon and took out a pack of butter, some of which I would mix with the salmon and potato when it was cooked. Then I opened a tin of premium cat food for Toby Jug.

Meanwhile, Lady May had wandered down to the sea and was playfully splashing about in the waves. Suddenly she surprised me by rolling full length in the sea the same way I had seen horses plunge about in rivers. It was a daring but obviously enjoyable antic, but when Toby Jug, after gobbling his breakfast, hastened down to the shore near her, I became worried that he would jump into the sea as well. I need not have worried as he simply stayed at the water's edge, watching her in between giving himself a thorough after-breakfast tongue-wash.

I brewed some coffee cowboy-style in a tin jug and ate my salmon mash with relish. It is amazing how sea air arouses the appetite and accentuates the taste.

Lady May left the sea and came to stand near me and started vigorously to shake herself dry, proving that my belief that horses are at times just like big dogs was all too true. Toby Jug played the sensible ploy of staying well away from the showering spray, but I took the brunt of it on my clean T-shirt.

Time to break camp, I thought, and led Lady May by

the halter over to a tree slightly upstream. There I tethered her and gave her a good grooming. After tidying the campsite, saddling the horse, packing the saddle bags and fitting Toby Jug into the papoose, it was late morning, but then we were on holiday so what did it matter? I rode the rest of the morning and the early afternoon at a fast trot and made the quarry car park at Craster by three in the afternoon.

I dismounted and tethered Lady May to a fence and loosened her cinch. There is a café there so I filled a pail of water to give her after she cooled down, but in the interim I let her graze on the grassy verge. In all of this I was watched by the café crowd with a mixture of curious amusement and incredulity. I kept the papoose on my back without unloading it because Toby was fast asleep inside.

I sat at a table outside in the sunshine and ate a pork pie with green salad and drank a mug of tea from the café. It was a welcome rest for me and the horse, and I whiled away the afternoon observing butterflies and bees taking nectar from the buddleia trees that were spaced about the small car park. When the café closed I waited for the car park to empty, took the pail of water for Lady May to have a drink as she rested in her corner, then tightened the cinch on her saddle and mounted up to continue the journey ahead.

I followed the road down to the small harbour, then swung left to pass the row of cottages facing the sea and go through the gate to pick up the track that ran alongside the rocky seashore. About a mile ahead I could make out the distinctive outline of the ruins of Dunstanburgh Castle looking ominously forbidding as the red glow of the setting sun touched its western ramparts. I bet that place has seen its share of blood-letting, I thought as we drew ever closer.

As we came near to the entrance to the castle grounds I felt a change in Lady May's demeanour, and then she commenced shaking her head up and down and snorting volubly. Finally, she stopped and would not go further. I knew enough about horses not to press her to go on but veered instead to the left to find a way around to the back of the castle. I had intended to seek a campsite on Castle Point, a jutting headland high above the rocky foreshore, but my horse flatly refused to go there.

There was no point in pursuing my original plan, so I resorted to a plan B and simply followed the coastal track until we reached the golden sands of Embleton Bay. Coursing around the sand dunes, I eventually chose a spot not far from a pillbox, a remnant of the Second World War defences. I pitched my tent and made camp on a grassy patch above a freshwater stream. I unsaddled Lady May and, after grooming her, I tied her to a boulder from a long tether, which permitted her to range along a strip of grassland suitable for grazing, not far from the road leading down to the bay.

There were several beach huts on the dunes fronting the sea, some of which were occupied by day-trippers. In the near distance I could tell there were two other horses tethered among the dunes, and now and again they called to Lady May, who ignored their greetings.

My tent was in a hollow shielded from the light wind from the sea. I freed Toby Jug from the papoose and put on his harness. As a cautionary measure I tethered him to one of the tent pegs since I could see several dogs in the distance enjoying the sands with their owners. I cleared a patch of dune grass and lit a fire with some driftwood I'd gathered and opened a tin of corned beef, which I would cook with some beans for my supper. Toby Jug was to have a tin of his favourite cat food before we settled down for the night.

Toby Jug was not happy about being tethered so I decided to give him a walk before we ate. I chose to walk the track back towards the castle since there were no signs of people or dogs there. Toby frisked ahead of me, pulling on his lead. He was glad to be moving since he'd been cooped up in the papoose all afternoon. As we drew closer to the castle I became aware of a change in the weather – dark, heavy clouds were moving in from the west and as the sun became obscured the air grew noticeably colder. It didn't take long to realize that a storm was brewing and rain was on the way. The view out to sea was grey and threatening and, to Toby's dismay, I cut short the walk and hurried back to our camp.

After quickly adding more wood to the fire, I tidied up the campsite by arranging the saddle and harness inside the tent – there wasn't much room but I did not want the gear to be exposed to the rain when the storm broke. I hustled up a plate of food for myself, which I ate standing up, facing out to sea. It was looking increasingly angry with tumultuous waves smashing against the shore and chasing all the casual walkers away to seek shelter. I made sure that Toby Jug had a dishful of cat meat with a sprinkling of his biscuits on top and a supply of water from the canteen.

Weatherwise things were now developing fast. Within a few moments the sea had started to surge and the wind was tearing at my tent with such ferocity that I had to secure the tent pegs deeper and tighten the guys to ensure that it wouldn't be blown away. Eating up in haste, I cleared everything away including Toby's things and huddled in the entrance of the tent, waiting for the onslaught of sleeting rain and gusting wind. Toby Jug had meanwhile found a niche near the back of the tent and was lying on my sleeping bag. He looked as miserable as I felt. The trip was beginning to reach a state of near disaster. What to do when the best-laid plans go awry?

Suddenly my discomfort was increased tenfold by an acute stinging sensation in my feet and ankles. I was wearing trainers and jeans, having rejected riding boots as too cumbersome for the trip. As I stripped off my trainers and socks I was surprised to find a cluster of ants streaming around my feet. They were in attack mode as I had obviously disturbed their nest when I pitched the tent. As their stings became more intense my only recourse was to abandon my shelter and stand outside in the pouring rain.

It was just as well I did so as Lady May appeared to be in the throes of a tantrum, stomping and whinnying and trying to escape her hobbles. She began to prance, rearing up on her back legs and shaking her head and mane in a wild fit of temper. With a storm-filled night stretching out ahead of me, an invasion of ants in my tent and an hysterical horse, things appeared to be going from bad to worse.

I tried to calm Lady May by talking softly to her and caressing her neck and back but she was frightened and momentarily inconsolable. I shortened the tether to her harness, freed the hobbles on her legs, which was made all the more difficult since she was jumping about so much that I became scared that she'd trample my feet. I decided to walk her around to try to calm her down.

I ended up leading a panicky horse by the halter around the approaches to Dunstanburgh Castle in the darkness to the accompaniment of claps of thunder and streaks of lightning. Adding to the macabre setting were flocks of wide-winged seagulls, probably fulmars, gliding overhead barely visible in the black sky and screaming their eerie calls on the howling wind. As I stared towards the towering ramparts, lashed by the storm, I could easily imagine that the brief shafts of light reflected in the glare of lightning were the unearthly apparitions for which the castle was notorious.

Lady May was not a happy horse and I was becoming fearful that in her nervous gyrations she would not only crush one of my feet with her steel hooves but wrench the lead rope from me and bolt off into the night. It can come as a surprise to any horse owner when their largely docile creature becomes an uncontrollable and formidable hulk of flesh weighing half a ton. In desperation I resorted to acting on a tip on how to deal with an over-excited horse from the Duke's groom at Alnwick Castle: I peeled off my new sweater, which was saturated anyway, and tied it around her head. The effect was instantaneous. Unable to see, she became a tad more biddable and I was able to turn her back towards the camp since I was worried about what would happen to Toby Jug if the ants in the tent attacked him.

On nearing the campsite I could see two glaring lights approaching along the wet beach. In moments I was joined by Barry and Jenny who had mounted a rescue attempt because of the worsening weather. Was I glad to see them? We wasted no time in talk but hastened to the campsite.

Jenny held a comparatively docile Lady May whilst I recovered Toby Jug, who had left the tent to find me. He was looking decidedly bedraggled and miserable, probably because the ants had also stung him. I became sure of this later when he kept scratching himself, which was unusual on his part. Securing him in the papoose and strapping it on my back, I took the lead and led Lady May towards the horsebox, which was parked adjacent to the beach. Barry dismantled the tent and carried it and the saddle bags whilst Jenny took care of the saddle and harness.

We soon reached the refuge of the huge horsebox and I led Lady May inside and tethered her in the stall. She was still trembling from her ordeal. Only then did I remove my wet sweater from her head. She immediately leaned forward and began eating some hay stacked in front of her.

I was soaked to the skin but glad to be out of the storm. As for Toby Jug, he was drenched as well. Jenny wrapped a blanket around me and persuaded me to sit up front in the cab with her and Barry, who was driving. A flask of hot sweet tea gave all of us, but especially me, some life-saving warmth as we sheltered from the gale outside. I felt uncomfortable in my wet clothing and longed for the comforts of home. Toby Jug seemed glad to be out of his rain-soaked papoose and lay on the floor of the cab, as close to the heater as he could manage.

The storm was still raging when we arrived at the paddock in Boulmer Haven. The wild roaring sea had completely engulfed the beach and was blowing sea spume in our faces as I led Lady May into the stable. She was quiet now despite the tempest. I saw to it that she had water and plenty of hay and then hugged and volubly thanked Jenny and Barry who were keen to be on their way home. I put the saddle and saddle bags, together with the rest of the detritus from our trip such as the tent and my sleeping bag, in the stable store.

Then I carried a subdued Toby Jug to the car where he immediately curled up on the passenger seat, as happy as I was to be going home. There and then I made a vow never to embark on another camping trip on horseback. This time I'd been fortunate to get out of it as easily as I did. It could have been a worse disaster for me, my cat and Lady May, and my imagination reeled with images of what could have happened.

Glad to be back at the cottage, I gave Toby Jug a quick bath in the sink and towelled him fluffy dry. Then I sank into a steaming bubble bath with a reviving hot cup of cocoa. Later, I heated a saucer of creamy milk for Toby after which we headed for bed and a good lie-in. Tomorrow would be time enough for the post-mortem on our trip, but for now it was sheer bliss to curl up in clean white sheets and to sleep the deep sleep of exhaustion after the turmoil we had suffered.

The morning after our ordeal in the storm dawned sunny and warm – such are the vicissitudes of weather. In spite of the exhaustion I had felt before going to bed, I found myself eager to rise and find what surprises this day would have in store for us. I cooked a hearty breakfast of fried eggs, bacon and some potato fritters. I separately prepared a plate of chicken livers for Toby Jug as a way of reviving his spirits. Notwithstanding our nightmarish experience of yesterday, soon we both seemed none the worse for wear.

There was much that needed attention at the cottage, but my first concern was for the horse, so Toby Jug and I lost no time in setting off for Boulmer. I need not have worried. When we arrived Jenny was already grooming Lady May, who was the picture of docility and patience. Jenny had called the vet. He had given her a thorough examination and announced that she was fit for purpose. Afterwards Jenny decided, in view of the calm and sunny weather, to take Lady May out for a ride on the beach. This was going to be the first time she had ridden her since she had called on my assistance. Whilst she was saddling her up, I left Toby Jug in the car and strolled over to the bar for a sandwich and a cool light beer.

I'd hardly had time to settle down with my drink when Jenny suddenly appeared looking dishevelled. She was unusually angry as I helped her to a seat and ordered her a drink. When she calmed down somewhat she told me that Lady May had bucked and thrown her off her back, and moreover had tried to kick and stomp her.

'It seems like she's a one-man horse and you're the man,'

she said, staring accusingly at me. Her experience brought to mind the trouble the two girls had when they'd tried to mount her. I told this to Jenny but I could see that she was really hurt, since she loved riding and had ridden horses all her life.

Leaving Jenny with a drink and the sympathetic company of Jack, her father-in-law, I felt obliged to check out Lady May. There she stood in a corner of the paddock looking all ruffled and with the saddle tilted in a lopsided angle on her back. I called softly to her and she whinnied back at me. She was probably feeling sorry for herself and I approached her cautiously. She didn't object when I removed her saddle and harness and followed behind me and then stood as I went through the paddock gate to the car where Toby Jug was freaking out with the frustration of not being included. I let him out and spent the next hour soothingly talking a cat and a horse back to a state of serenity.

Jenny waved to me as she came out of the bar without speaking and drove off in her Land Rover. I wondered if she might still be upset at Lady May's reaction to her. Anyway, time will tell, I thought, and I fully expected that she would be in contact with me in the next few days, but nothing came. Meanwhile, I left a calmed horse in the company of an unruffled cat perched on the paddock fence as I headed for the bar and my unfinished drink and sandwich. When I looked back, both animals were nose to nose, no doubt consoling each other, and for the moment peace reigned supreme all around.

I had lots to do at the cottage to get things straight

and knew that others would be caring for Lady May as regards feeding and grooming so it would be convenient to leave her in peace for a few days. It was bright summer weather and the grass was growing lush after the rainstorm so there would be plenty to interest her in the paddock.

Back at home there was much washing to take care of and the plants in the greenhouse needed attention. Toby Jug was obviously glad to be back home and joined me in whatever I was doing, whether it was hanging out the washing to dry or pruning tomato and cucumber plants in the greenhouse. He was revelling in the close contact with me and, of course, his attachment was a pleasure as I went about the business of caring for our domestic living.

It was several days before I had the spare time to visit Lady May, and when I did I was in for a shock: she wasn't there. Instead there were two donkeys in the paddock. On making enquiries at the pub I learned that Jenny had taken Lady May back to the farm. There was no message for me. I realized that Jenny had the right to take Lady May – it was her horse – but I suspected that there was a hidden agenda. I surmised that there was an element of jealousy in her action and decided to let the situation rest for the moment. Toby Jug would not leave until he had checked that the stable was empty too and that his friend Lady May really had gone.

I decided that there was nothing I could do, short of confronting Jenny about what had happened, so in a disturbed mood I returned to the cottage.

Toby Jug and I resumed our normal holiday-period

routine of gardening and going for walks by the river, but in the back of my mind I began to worry about Lady May. Jenny's behaviour was her responsibility and it was no business of mine, except that she had asked me for help, which I had more than willingly given. Now I was being excluded from contact with a horse of whom I had grown especially fond. It was not courteous and I felt hurt. Days passed into weeks but there was no word.

Then one Sunday night a loud banging at the front door jerked me out of a deep sleep and at first I didn't know where I was. I had fallen asleep reading Alistair MacLean's *HMS Ulysses* and for a brief moment I thought I was on a stricken ship which had just been torpedoed. I switched on the light and checked the time in a daze – just after 2 a.m. It was the middle of August and the sky was still dark. Wondering who it could be at that time, I opened the door to find Barry looking desperately stressed as he blurted out his message:

'Lady May collapsed yesterday and we cannot get her up again. The vet has been and said that her heart has given out and there is nothing to be done except to put her to sleep. Jenny is very upset and thought you might like to see her before she dies.' My stomach turned sour and my heart started racing at the news.

'I'll be there directly,' I said, to his evident relief. After he had gone, I sat a moment to digest the news.

'God only knows what that horse has suffered,' I said aloud. As I washed and dressed, a sleepy-eyed Toby Jug joined me downstairs. He gave me a questioning look.

'I know what you're thinking,' I said to him. 'But we

have an emergency on our hands. Lady May is dying and needs us.'

He seemed to grasp the meaning of my words and certainly picked up the sentiment of despair in my voice as, without demur, he followed me out to the car.

When we arrived, Barry was waiting as I carried Toby from the car. He led me straight over to the large loosebox where Lady May lay, and my heart sank at the sight of her. She was lying stretched out on the straw and she tried to lift her head when she heard me greet her. Toby Jug immediately ran to her side and started licking her face as I knelt down by her head and began stroking her neck and softly murmuring sweet talk to her. As I cuddled her head she suddenly began to make snuffling noises which I thought were due to something choking her, until I realized she was sobbing and her eyes were wet with tears.

Toby Jug kept licking her forehead as I gently stroked her and wondered what to do to console and cheer her. I suddenly had the idea of singing to her, and so I began to sing a tune which would be familiar because she had heard it many times when we were out riding. It was a cowboy song called 'Home on the Range'. I hoped it would soothe her and she'd be reassured that I had not forgotten her and would stay as long she wanted.

I don't know how long we lay there, but there came a point where Lady May cried out in a rasping whicker and then she gave an almighty shudder and was gone. Toby Jug stopped licking her and I stopped singing. We both knew she was dead. Toby Jug began to wail and I buried my face in her silky mane and wept. At some point Jenny appeared, her face all tear-stained, and she began gnawing at a fist clamped to her mouth as she agonized over what had happened.

I gathered up Toby Jug, who was reluctant to leave his friend's body, and I whispered a last 'Goodbye, love' to my horse, because to all intents and purposes she had been my horse and I knew she had grown to love me. Her passing broke my heart and I felt guilty that I had not challenged Jenny for taking her away from me, but I'd thought that things would work out all right. Lady May had needed me and Toby and I had let her down by not pursuing her to the farm. I felt terrible and I could tell that Toby Jug was upset. He had already been through a lot in his short life and now he had lost a close friend.

I could find no words for Jenny as I struggled to manage my own sorrow. Notwithstanding the vet's diagnosis of heart failure, I believed that Lady May also died of a broken heart because she believed that I'd abandoned her.

One day soon I would drive to Boulmer and carve her name large on the chestnut tree she liked to stand under as a memorial to an exceptional horse. She would not be forgotten.

I felt drained of feeling, and when we got home I played a lot of Puccini and Verdi over the next few days to try and salve the emotional wounds I felt over the dreadful business. The picture of Lady May haunted my mind and would not leave me, no matter what I did. I would never forget her. Toby Jug and I comforted each other, listened to the music and went for long walks in the woods.

* * *

After a while, I felt the need to get right away to restore my spirits. Impulsively, I decided to make a trip there and then. I packed the minimum essentials for the trip, filling a kitbag with waterproof clothing, and picking up my hiking boots and my maps of the Lake District.

Before leaving I called on Laura, a neighbour, and asked if she would feed Toby Jug and let him into the cottage at night. I intended to 'rough it' for a couple of days without putting him to any trouble because where I was going would not suit him. I stroked and fondled him and said I'd be back soon but I just had to get away on my own to sort out the devils in my mind. Toby knew Laura as she was a friend of ours, so there would be no problem there. I left the keys to the cottage with her and showed her the cupboard containing tins of cat food. As I sped away, in the rear-view mirror I could see Toby Jug sending me off from his vantage point high in the old apple tree.

As I drove across country and down the M6 towards the Lake District I churned over the events of the last few months. Animals meant a great deal to me. Without them I would have felt bereft of companionship and love. Toby Jug played a large part in making my life feel meaningful, and Lady May had become a significant part of it too.

Now the balance had been upset by her death and had left me feeling vulnerable, so I needed to find a way to cope with the loss. I was headed for a high place in the hills to draw upon nature's reservoir of energy. Nature has a way of restoring the damaged self after a bereavement, and I needed that now.

I turned off the motorway and veered onto the winding road for Ullswater. I drove along the lakeside to the village of Glenridding and parked my car. Shouldering my backpack, I headed straight up the steep stony track past the youth hostel and onward as the pointed summit of Catstycam came into view. Beyond lay the huge bulk of Helvellyn rising to over 3,000 feet.

It was hot work climbing the last few feet to reach the table-top summit of Helvellyn itself, and I needed to pause a while to catch my breath. There is something alluring about the top of a mountain, especially the sense of freedom that comes with the achievement of reaching the top. The air tastes fresher, the views are breathtaking and the expanse of sky above is all-enveloping. There wasn't a cloud in the blue sky and I just felt I had to lie down and let all the natural wonder of the place seep into me.

Later, while I walked around the mountain to enjoy the views, I came upon a man sitting smoking in the front of a small tent. He hailed me and invited me to join him. He offered me a drink of white wine in a plastic cup, which I found most refreshing. He introduced himself as an academic lecturer, so we had much in common and we exchanged first names. He remarked that he was amazed to find midges, those small flying insects with an irritating bite, at that height, and was smoking a cigar to keep them away. We talked for a while but, as it was late afternoon, I needed to move on.

I left him to continue my way across the mountain, which I intended to descend on the other side. This turned out to be a reckless decision. All went well at first until

I reached a precipitous part of the track along a narrow ridge known as Striding Edge. Perhaps I was becoming tired and, with everything else on my mind, I wasn't concentrating sufficiently, but I stumbled, lost my balance and tumbled over the edge. It felt like a long way down as I crashed repeatedly into rocky outcrops. I felt my ribs break on the way down and, with a severe blow to my head, lost consciousness.

I awoke through a haze of pain to the sensation of a dog licking my face. The dog, a black Labrador, belonged to a man and woman who happened to be hiking at ground level and had seen me fall. They helped me to my feet and gave me a drink of water from a flask. They could see I was still dizzy and hurt so, when I could move, they insisted on helping me down the rest of the way to my car, which was parked near their own.

There they administered first aid for the wound to my head, which had started to bleed. They wanted to send for an ambulance but I persuaded them not to. They did insist, however, that I accompany them to a café where they bought me a strong, sweet, milky coffee, after which I felt sufficiently revived to set off for home. I thanked the couple profusely and put on a show of masking my pain so as not to worry them.

I had originally intended to stay the night somewhere in Glenridding, but now I just longed to get home as quickly as possible. The drive back was a nightmare because I could only use my left hand since I had injured my right shoulder and had little feeling in my arm. I thought at times I would pass out with the pain, but hours later I pulled into the yard of the cottage and there was the welcome sight of Toby Jug to greet me.

I limped thankfully into the refuge of my cottage and sank into the armchair by the fire, which I didn't have the energy to light. I sat nursing a large drink of brandy and, with Toby purring on my knee, I fell deeply asleep.

The next thing I knew was my neighbour Laura bending over me with an anxious expression on her face. It was 7.30 in the morning and I had slept the night away. Laura had come to feed Toby when she saw my car and realized I was back. After hearing a brief account from me and seeing the state I was in, she immediately ran to the telephone box at the end of the street and tried to summon the village doctor. The advice from the surgery was that I needed hospital treatment, and eventually an ambulance was called.

When the ambulance arrived I found that I was still so sore that I couldn't stand up. The ambulance men were very professional. They strapped me into a chair-like contraption, fitted me with an oxygen mask and I was duly carted off to the Royal Victoria Infirmary in Newcastle upon Tyne. An abiding memory for me as I was being lifted into the back of the ambulance was the sight of Toby Jug standing by the feet of Laura, watching me. He looked desperate. I could tell, although I couldn't hear him, that he was whining in torment at me being taken from him. I was glad that Laura would look after him in my absence.

Once I was admitted to hospital my great number of cuts and bruises were patched up and I was put on a saline drip. My right shoulder was dislocated and for this

I received the expert attention of a large, specialist nurse, who after examining me said that she needed to slip my shoulder back into its socket and that it would hurt.

'It already hurts,' I replied, but she took hold of my arm, fitted a piece of leather between my teeth and told me to bite down hard on it. Then she proceeded to wrench and jam the limb back in place. A shaft of pain unlike anything I had ever felt before suffused my consciousness and I fainted.

I came to later, lying in bed in a hospital ward. My right shoulder was strapped in tight bandaging and my arm was in a sling. I was given a cup of tea by the night-duty nurse and a cocktail of different drugs including a strong dose of antibiotics. After this, I lay back and slept the deep sleep of exhaustion.

I was not a good patient and kept complaining that I wished to go home. Unfortunately my fall had contributed to a chest infection, which had probably lain latent since the soaking I'd endured on the camping trip with Lady May. I spent almost two weeks in hospital before I was pronounced fit enough to be sent home. My ribs were cracked in several places but they were left to heal on their own without binding, which was fine except that the slightest movement, including a cough or sneeze, sent pain shooting through my chest.

A hospital minibus at last delivered me to the door of the cottage. Laura saw me arrive and hastened over to see if I needed any help. I thanked her for looking after things and then, in mounting alarm, asked the whereabouts of Toby Jug.

'I'm sorry but I don't know. He disappeared about two days ago and before then he just seemed to spend his time between watching out for you from the top of the apple tree and lying on your bed. He hasn't eaten anything as far as I know for the last four days. He seemed to be pining for you and wouldn't be consoled. My husband and I searched everywhere but couldn't find him. So sorry to have to tell you this,' she finished, quietly.

I thanked her for all she had done, but my heart went into overdrive at the news. After Laura left I stood outside in the yard and whistled and called for Toby Jug but still there was no sign of him. I searched around the garden in case he was lying under a bush but failed to find any trace of him. Eventually I combed the house thinking that perhaps he was hiding under a bed or in a cupboard, but still no Toby Jug.

At last I thought of the old outhouse and ventured inside to hunt for him. To my relief I found him lying in a dark corner, but he looked in a sorry state of abandon and despair. He whimpered as I picked him up and cuddled him in my arms even though my ribs seared with pain. I carried him lovingly into the cottage and gave him a careful brush and comb because he was in desperate need of grooming. Cats are normally fastidious about their appearance but Toby looked scruffy as if he had given up all hope of ever seeing me again and it seemed as if he'd retreated into the outhouse to die.

As I stroked and spoke to him he revived, but he fussed around me just to make absolutely sure it was me in the flesh. It had been a great shock for him to view me being carted away, all trussed up in the ambulance chair. Usually when I had to go away for a few days I have left him at my mother's house and he knew the routine. I had disappeared twice in quick succession and had been missing for a fortnight. He probably believed that I wasn't coming back, just like Lady May. I had let my beloved Toby Jug down by going off on a wild trip without him and injured myself in the process. I had a lot to make up to him and I began to try to set things right straightaway.

The cottage had a forsaken appearance and, although my arm was still in a sling and my shoulder wasn't fit for purpose, I managed to light the fire and decided to cook an appetizing meal for us both. First, I would need supplies. Toby Jug dogged my heels like a limpet. Not only did he follow me into the garage, he was first in the car. Obviously I was going nowhere without him. I drove into the main street of Felton and bought a large sirloin steak from the butcher, followed by milk and bread from the local shop. I also called on Laura to tell her that I'd found Toby Jug and I gave her a bunch of flowers and a box of chocolates from my shopping trip.

Back home, I soon had the steak sizzling away in my large frying pan with some potatoes, carrots and a few onions. We sat together as per usual with Toby Jug opposite me on his chair at the table and with his share of the steak cut into small chunks on his plate. We ate a delicious meal. Toby eschewed the vegetables but devoured his steak. He was really hungry.

When done, we sat together by the fire, happy to be reunited, and listened to Tchaikovsky's 'The Sleeping

Beauty'. As the music and the fire died away, two sleepy heads mounted the stairs for bed and the homecoming was complete. After an enforced absence from home there's nothing to equal the bliss of sleeping once more in one's own bed.

As I snuggled between the sheets with the comforting weight of Toby Jug around my ankles I reflected that an important time in my life had come and gone. I had survived to live another day so I should be prepared now for whatever new experiences the future would bring. Whilst in hospital I dreamt that I was riding Lady May along a golden beach with the sunset turning the sky and the sea an orange hue. I was so happy that when I awoke in the bare, sterile hospital ward I cried. I missed the companionship of that horse, and because of a foolish whim I had nearly lost my cat as well. No one's life is a bed of roses, but when a pet dies or is lost, the result is always traumatic. I shall forever miss Lady May. Whenever I see someone out riding on a beach or over fields I feel a deep pang of remorse coupled with envy.

Over the next few weeks I gradually regained my health and strength and a new episode opened up in the lives of Toby Jug and me.

ALL AT SEA

The coastal areas and seascapes of Northumberland are unrivalled for their natural beauty. The country adjacent to the castle at Bamburgh is especially enchanting and has been much favoured by artists and filmmakers alike. The bay at Beadnell I find most to my liking. Feeling at a loose end with the rest of the summer stretching out before me, I made several trips there to wander along the beach and investigate the rock pools for sealife when the tide was out.

Toby Jug was in his element, sniffing each fresh patch of seaweed and driftwood we found. He loved to hover at the side of the pools left in the rocky crevices, crouching in cat-stealth mode as he watched the movement of sand eels and miniature crabs that inhabited the depths.

I always kept him on a tight lead at such times, as I was mindful of people walking their dogs. I also carried a stout stick with me as a deterrent to any dog which came too close. I love dogs but I love my cat more. I had a strategy that if we were attacked I would swing Toby up into my arms my means of the lead attached to his harness. Fortunately no such crisis ever occurred as the dogs we encountered at the beach were too busy chasing balls, sticks and each other to notice us. When the dog population became too numerous and the tide was in, we retreated to the high dunes fringing the beach and from this elevated position we could gaze out upon the vista of sea and sky.

On one such trip I met an acquaintance who later became a friend. He was called Lionel and I had first met him at a school at Rothbury where he was headmaster. I recognized him as soon as I caught sight of him standing at the water's edge preparing a boat to go sailing. He waved and invited me to join him. His boat was a clinker-built Enterprise sailing dinghy and there was ample room inside for both of us and Toby Jug. There was a light, freshening breeze that morning as we made several circuits around the bay.

For me it was an exhilarating experience that awakened a desire for more, and Lionel offered to teach me to sail. Toby Jug, however, appeared to have mixed feelings about sailing and kept looking at me and whining during the sailing manoeuvres, particularly when he was splashed with seawater as the dinghy turned and changed tack. I stroked him and told him to try to enjoy the experience, otherwise I would leave him at home the next time. Clever cat that he was, he seemed to get the message.

Later in the week I joined Lionel for my first lesson. Toby Jug hugged my side like a shadow as we crossed the sand towards the water's edge where the sailing dinghy lay all ready for us. Lionel first of all talked us through a few safety procedures. I donned a life jacket and, accompanied by Toby Jug, climbed aboard the fifteen-foot boat.

Just before we pushed off from the beach, I attached a

large inflatable armband – the kind children wear at the swimming baths – to Toby's harness to keep him afloat in case we took a dunking.

It was a glorious morning and the seaside setting evoked memories of those rapturous days of childhood when I was first taken on trips to the beach. It's the scents as much as the views that arouse such memories – dank seaweed and wet sand together with the salty taste of spray on our lips. I particularly remember the taste of sand in my mouth as I stood as a child looking out to sea and eating a tomato sandwich given to me by my mother. The sand came from my fingers as I had been building a sandcastle. The cries of gulls as they wheeled close to shore and the sound of the waves helped exert a powerful urge within us to put out to sea and become part of it.

Without a word spoken, Lionel and I launched the boat into the gentle swell. There was hardly a whiff of wind as we drifted on the tide. The sails hung motionless in the hot sunlight as the boat lay becalmed, and all we could hear was the rhythmic murmur of the water lapping against the sides of the boat. It was another rare moment to savour.

'Let's see if we can find the breeze, there's sure to be one further out,' said Lionel, handing me a spare paddle, and we paddled the craft towards a horizon lost in misty haze. I sat on the bench by the tiller and Lionel took prime place in the bow where he could handle the sails. Toby Jug rested by my side, having a catnap snooze, but I knew that he wasn't all that happy to be at sea. I could feel that he was on edge and keeping a wary eye on the proceedings.

All at once we had a visitor. A seabird with a wide wing-span. Probably a gannet, I speculated, as it circled the boat inspecting what we were doing.

'It's a herring gull,' Lionel corrected me. 'It wants to know if we're catching any fish.'

Just to be sure it wasn't missing anything, the gull swooped in a low pass over us, calling stridently, then flew off out of sight in the huge sweep of sky. As my paddle disturbed the surface of the sea, rays of sunlight penetrated the water and revealed a shoal of tiny silver fish. Deeper down I could see dark forms with flashes of silver moving over the rocks beneath the boat. Noticing my interest, Toby Jug ventured to look over the side of the dinghy too and was so fascinated by the sight of the sea creatures that I feared he might jump in. I tightened my grip on his harness lead as he continued to peer into the depths.

We paddled for a while longer in search of wind, but it was an exceptionally still morning with a singular beauty rare to the Northumberland coast. The conditions reminded me of tales of huge Tudor galleons drifting becalmed on windless seas, waiting for wind to move them on. We ceased paddling and just sat back to enjoy ourselves and savour the moment. Nothing lasts forever and at last our patience was rewarded by the onset of a light breeze. It began from far out to sea as we detected a slight ruffling of the water's surface, as the air began to move and nudged our sails to life. We started the business of sailing, with our craft driving its bow into the emerging wavelets. We picked up speed and sailed smoothly ahead, crossing and re-crossing Beadnell Bay.

We spent an exhilarating morning and I learned the skills and tactics of handling the dinghy under sail. I enjoyed every moment, but I'm afraid that Toby Jug had a largely miserable time huddled close to my side. I decided not to subject him to this experience again.

We beached the boat, disassembled the sails, and I carried Toby up the sandy beach to the car park. I left him to curl up for a restorative siesta on the back seat of the car but was careful to open all four windows just wide enough to allow a cross current to cool the interior. Back at the beach I helped Lionel to drag the dinghy across the line of dunes to its place outside his caravan.

Whilst Lionel was making the boat secure I drove into the nearby town of Seahouses and bought a take-away meal of fish and chips for us all from the Neptune Restaurant on the main street. By the time I returned with the food, Toby Jug had revived and was able to join us in Lionel's caravan for the meal.

Relaxing in the cosy caravan gave me an idea. I'd observed that there were a number of small caravans adjacent to the beach that were on offer for summer rental. Acting on a sudden impulse, I hired one for a month for Toby Jug and me. It proved to be a good move since the fine weather continued unabated throughout the time we spent there.

The change of location and scenery did us both good and I was pleased to see how Toby adapted to caravan living. He seemed especially to enjoy the views through the large windows, excitedly watching the antics of rabbits feeding at evening and early morning. He also delighted in having the constant company of myself, except for the few times I joined Lionel for some sailing lessons.

During our stay, I took advantage of Seahouses as a fishing port and we ate fresh fish every day. Sometimes it was sea trout poached in full cream milk, or juicy fried cod from the fish restaurant, or fat, succulent oak-smoked kippers from Craster which I purchased from the Olde Ship Hotel overlooking Seahouses harbour. The hotel was distinctive for its bar, which had an engaging aura of bygone days when fishermen and seafarers drank their rum and ale at the antique polished wooden counter. The dark interior was festooned with salvaged items from old ships, including huge lanterns, ships' wheels, barometers and clocks together with fishing nets adorned with cork floats hanging from the wooden ceiling. Models of ships in glass cases were fixed to the walls along with framed photographs of long-dead boat crews. The place reminded me of Robert Louis Stevenson's *Treasure Island*.

One sunny morning Lionel called for me at our caravan in a highly excited state. He'd heard from some fishermen that sardine shoals were running close inshore and he reckoned that if we launched the boat quickly enough we might be able to catch a few. With a hasty goodbye to Toby Jug I lost no time in helping to manhandle the little sailing craft down to the water's edge. There was a fair wind ruffling the surface of the sea as Lionel dressed the sails and then we launched into the waves.

Lionel sat in the stern steering and handling the sails whilst I was given the job of sorting through a workbox of fishing gear to assemble what was needed. Sardines tend to feed near the surface so we would not require heavy weights – just enough to carry our feathered hooks a few feet below the surface.

We headed out to sea away from the inshore rocks, and lo and behold we soon sighted a flock of screaming sea-gulls swooping and diving as they fed.

'They've found the sardines,' Lionel said. 'Let's join them.'

We headed their way as fast as our sails could bear us and in no time at all we were above the fast-moving shoals. I knew it was time to let out the fishing lines and so I sat midship and held fast to a line on each side of the dinghy. Almost at once I felt the tug of the lines as fish were caught and I was kept busy reeling in each line and unhooking three or four of the large, beautiful, dark blue and silver fish at a time. Meanwhile, Lionel sailed with expert ease as we beat back and forth across the area. Soon I had a bucket-load of fish and it was time to head towards the shore. As we sailed in, a couple of small fishing boats arrived from Seahouses and took up where we left off. It had been an exhilarating two hours.

The tide was fully in so we didn't have far to drag the boat, which was just as well because we both felt exhausted after our efforts of the morning. I invited Lionel to my caravan for coffee and carried the heavy bucket contain-ing our catch to show Toby Jug. The sight and smell of the fish had him mesmerized as he circled, sniffed and pawed at the sardines. Once or twice he looked up searchingly at me and whined for an explanation, which caused us both to laugh.

'How should we cook them?' I asked.

'We'll barbecue them on long steel prongs like they do in Spain and Greece. We'll do them tonight on my small barbecue,' Lionel said, and that's what we did.

I had never tasted fish like them. They were so fresh the flesh fell apart in my mouth and I watched with great satisfaction as Toby Jug demolished his share. My previous experiences of sardines were of small tins of tiny fish immersed in sauce, which I had eaten on buttered toast. They were delicious but not a patch on the fish we caught that day. These large fish were a revelation to me and they tasted so sweet they were a meal fit for a gourmet.

'There's nothing to beat fresh fish you've caught yourself and cooked however you like it,' said Lionel, summing up the day. Added to this was the satisfaction of watching Toby Jug experience his first taste of fresh fish straight from the sea.

Some of the other exquisite experiences I had when sailing that summer were on hot days when we were becalmed two or three miles offshore. We would anchor the boat by letting out a long rope wrapped around a large stone Lionel normally used as ballast in the boat. Then we would slip over the side and have a luxurious swim, keeping as near to the boat as possible in case the current carried us away. The experience of swimming out at sea was phenomenally exciting because there was no land in immediate reach and the depth of the sea at that point was unknown. The water was ecstatically cool beneath the surface and yet soothingly warm in the sunlight. No rich man on his million-dollar yacht could have had it better. We sometimes took it in turns to have a swim but when we were both in the sea we agreed that one of us should at all times hold onto the anchor rope.

One blazing hot afternoon when I'd finished my morning sailing lesson I took Toby Jug with me in the car for a trip to Bamburgh Castle. On the way through Seahouses I stopped to buy a pack of gourmet ice cream from Coxon's ice-cream parlour and a large punnet of strawberries from a market stall. By the time we reached Bamburgh it was roasting hot in the car, and after parking behind the castle I slipped the harness and lead on Toby Jug, and, carrying the ice cream and strawberries, headed for a shaded spot on the beach.

There I portioned out a large share of ice cream into Toby's bowl, which I always carried in the car, and served myself strawberries and ice cream in the large cup of my flask. Toby Jug was stunned at first by the cold taste of the ice cream and looked across at me as if to ask, 'Is this okay for me to eat?' When he saw me tucking in, he buried his muzzle in the bowl and relished the icy sensation. I ate mine so fast that I experienced yet again what is commonly called an 'ice-cream headache', which a doctor friend once told me was known medically as 'cryogenic cephalgia'.

We enjoyed a couple of hours on the sands watching yachts far out to sea and I reminisced about other times when this whole area of Alnwick and Bamburgh had provided me with some extra-special memories. Now Toby was a grown-up little cat, I wanted him to know all the details of our shared history, so just like I had recently told him the tale of first discovering him in the barn, I told him the tale of why the very sands of Bamburgh we were stretching out on right now were important to our story.

Even though day-to-day living tended to take on a monotonous aspect, and many people might think Northumberland is a sleepy, uneventful place to live, I had found the whole area ripe with surprising events and adventures ever since the early sixties, when I graduated from university and was appointed to a teaching post in Northumberland.

Back then I was living in lodgings near Alnwick and it was my habit to have an evening meal on Fridays at the White Swan in town before returning home. At that time the White Swan was an archaic building, which appealed to my fascination for older buildings. Leading to the hotel bar was a narrow, dark-wood panelled corridor, undoubtedly of Jacobean origin. I also admired the bar room itself, with its long, polished oak bar counter and antique panelling that were a feat of excellent craftsmanship. At each end of the narrow room a coal fire added a homely touch of comfort and I enjoyed many an end of the working week having a plate of chicken sandwiches and a pot of hot coffee with cream there.

One Friday evening, as I bustled along the Jacobean corridor, I was suddenly confronted by two burly men who pushed me back. An altercation ensued, and just as I was about to be thrown out of the hotel, the passage door to the bar was flung open. A familiar face emerged and demanded an explanation.

'Sorry, Mr Burton,' one of the men said, 'but this little guy tried to bust his way in.'

I stared in shock at the well-known countenance of Richard Burton, international star of stage and screen.

Just as I was about to mumble an apology, he suddenly put his arm around my shoulders and simply said, in his unmistakably rich voice, 'Well, let the little bugger in then.'

Still disturbed by the confrontation with these two burly men, the hotel was the last place I wanted to be, but I was ushered into the inner sanctum of the bar where another familiar face was sitting slumped on a stool, drink in hand. I recognized him immediately: it was Peter O'Toole. I was manoeuvred to sit between these two modern-day icons and I was prevailed upon to tell them my life story, such as it was.

To tell the truth, I don't think they listened to a word. They were both so inebriated. There was no barman present and so Richard Burton himself poured me a glass of malt whisky from a range of bottles he had to hand on the bar. I only took minute sips of this drink since I had to drive to my lodgings on an empty stomach. After an hour or so had passed I excused myself and left, doubting whether they even realized I was leaving.

Whilst the famous guests had been far from communicative, I found the night porter manning the reception desk more than willing to talk. He told me that the two men were in the area to film a story about Thomas Becket when he was Archbishop of Canterbury. Burton played the part of Becket and O'Toole was King Henry II. The loquacious porter reeled off a host of other famous names who were taking part in the production, including John Gielgud, another actor I had long admired. Leaning over the desk in a conspiratorial manner, he whispered his latest news: in the morning the actors were to play an important scene on Bamburgh beach behind the castle.

When I told my colleagues at school that I had been in the company of Peter O'Toole and Richard Burton, they laughingly scoffed at me as if I were spinning a yarn. The experience, however, had a profound effect on me.

The following morning I arose bright and early and travelled to Bamburgh. The area was overrun with the vans and large coaches of the film company. There were technicians everywhere, erecting massive lights to aim at the beach area, and there were thick cables which snaked across the road and along the footpaths carrying electric power to the lights and cameras. The road down to the old town had been blocked off by police barriers so I was parked a fair distance from the beach. Indeed, the whole picturesque little village of Bamburgh had been taken over by the Hollywood film industry.

Wending my way through the crowd of people and avoiding tripping over cables was no mean feat, but at last I had a clear view from the top of the sand dunes. The entrance to the beach side of the castle had been altered by the addition of some cleverly designed structures that gave it the appearance of a French chateau. At each end of the beach I could see groups of horsemen carrying what seemed to be halberds with colourful V-shaped flags fluttering in the wind.

I waited along with a small army of onlookers and

technicians for whatever was meant to happen next. The morning sun blazed down from a clear blue sky, but even that light was not sufficient because suddenly the huge lights were switched on to further illuminate the beach. A stentorian male voice bellowed the word 'Action' through a megaphone, at the sound of which a horseman from the right emerged in a full gallop to meet a sedate procession of riders from the left. I was witnessing my companion of the night before, Richard Burton, meeting the English king, played by Peter O'Toole, for a reconciliation.

Then with surprising speed the formidable mass of equipment was dismantled, the actors vanished and, with thunderous roars, the huge vehicles and all the personnel disappeared. The little town of Bamburgh was able to return to the tranquillity for which it is famous, only slightly ruffled by the Hollywood invasion. A few years later I was able to view the same scene on the silver screen when the film *Becket* was shown at a local cinema.

Years later, sitting on the beach with Toby Jug, I enjoyed telling my little cat all about the filming, but I gathered that he wasn't really interested. However, the experience had caused a sea change in my attitude towards the area. I realized that the reason why Hollywood had turned up on our doorstep was because the area was so special. Northumberland had a natural enchantment all of its own. As well as its castles and stately homes, it had wild valleys like Ingram, remote hills like Cheviot, winding rivers and a beautiful coastline. I decided there and then that I would prefer to make my home here in a rural setting, ideally an ancient cottage.

Strange to say, my wishes were realized quicker than I expected when I secured an appointment at Alnwick College, and before too long found the home I wanted in the hamlet of West Thirston. As I relaxed on the beach at Bamburgh with Toby Jug, I reflected on how, arising from that incident at the White Swan in Alnwick, I had found the job and the cottage of my dreams. Furthermore, if I hadn't lived at Owl Cottage, I would never have had the good fortune to find my beloved cat, Toby Jug.

Talking to Toby Jug that day made me realize how far I had progressed from a troubled childhood, and I recalled how determined I had been to win the qualifications to open the doors to a new life, which would eventually involve a lovely old cottage and a tremendous young cat. I stroked my little companion and repeated once more how much he meant to me as he stretched lengthwise on the warm sand. It was late evening when we returned to the caravan and ate more grilled sardines for supper.

When it was dark I led Toby Jug on one of our nightly walks across the sand dunes in the moonlight. Life was good, I mused in the large caravan bed with Toby at my feet. The feelings of cosy wellbeing were accentuated during the night by the drumming of rain on the hard caravan roof, which induced a soothing sleepiness. It had been another special day to savour.

Towards the end of our holiday, we also made a trip by car over to nearby Holy Island, where I had taken Toby Jug during his first year. We walked around the outside of the gaunt old castle, which always gave me the impression of foreboding as well as turbulent times past. I wondered about how the island had fared in Viking raids when the Norsemen overran Northumbria. Toby Jug was blissfully unaware of such issues as he playfully investigated every rocky pool we encountered on our walk. He appeared to thoroughly enjoy the visit, as I did, and seemed disappointed when, all too soon, we had to head back to the mainland to avoid being marooned on the island by the encroaching tide.

At the end of our month's stay in the caravan I found it quite a wrench to depart from Beadnell and leave behind sun-filled mornings in the company of Lionel. I had fond memories of warm summer winds propelling our boat through the waters, of eating fish fresh from the sea and of whole afternoons spent lazily snoozing on the warm sand. I even thought about buying a small sailing dinghy for myself, but the idea soon dimmed when I realized that Toby Jug was never likely to want to be involved. The idea of having a caravan at Beadnell stayed with me, however, but I'm sad to say I never did anything about it.

THE RAVEN AND THE WITCH OF RAMPTON HALL

When I returned to the cottage from our month-long caravan holiday there was much to do. The garden, even in the short time I had been away, was overgrown and in dire need of attention. Toby Jug immediately resumed his semi-wild forays around the local gardens but surprisingly spent an inordinate amount of time shadowing me. It was as if he was worried that I might run off without him. After a full day toiling in the wilderness I headed indoors for a rest and recuperation.

Recently I had strained my finances to pay for a much-needed electric shower to be installed within the old bathroom of the cottage. As I luxuriated in the deliciously hot water, washing away the strains of tired muscles, I became aware of a figure pressed up against the outside of the cubicle. It was Toby Jug. Although I had given him a gentle wash in the shower whenever his fur was muddy, I couldn't believe that he now wanted to join me in the powerful shower and decided against letting him in.

Whilst towelling myself dry I realized something was wrong. Toby kept mewing up at me and running forwards and backwards from the room as if there was an urgent need for me to attend to an emergency. I dressed quickly and followed him out into the garden. I saw at once what was bothering him. In a far corner of the garden, under the spread of a young beech tree, a dark-coloured creature was floundering about. As I drew near I saw that it was a bird, black as a crow, but larger.

Here I go again, I thought, as it seemed my destiny to always be caring for disabled creatures of one kind or another. Only this was no ordinary bird. I guessed it was a raven; it was injured and obviously unable to fly as one of its wings was fanned out to favour its left side. It had probably been shot, I realized, once I spotted specks of dried blood. Silently I cursed the countryman's philosophy of killing anything that appeared to threaten income from pheasant and grouse rearing.

The bird didn't seem at all distressed at my presence and allowed me to pick it up and carry it inside the cottage. I set it down on a chair in the kitchen whilst I spread newspaper across the bench and filled a bowl with warm water and a few drops of an antiseptic solution. As I examined the raven I was surprised at how docile it was – the bird was obviously a domesticated pet accustomed to human contact. Surprisingly, it also had no apparent fear of Toby Jug who, of course, lingered near me as I attended to the bird's injuries.

The raven was beautiful with a healthy blue-black sheen to its feathers, and it distressed me immensely to find several shotgun pellets embedded in its side. Swabbing the wound with antiseptic solution, I prised out four pellets from the wound, during which time the creature watched me intently with a clear-eyed gaze. I dressed the wound with healing ointment and placed the bird as comfortably as I could on a blanket remnant in a cardboard box and hoped for the best.

I had managed to ladle a drink of water down its beak but decided to leave further resuscitation to nature as I placed the box on the hearth near the fireplace. I would soon be lighting the fire, but for now the raven was in the warmest place in the cottage. Meanwhile, Toby Jug, who had been in watchful attendance all during my ministrations, seemed satisfied now that I had responded to his alarums. I praised him, saying, 'Well done Toby!' accompanied by lots of strokes.

I was very much aware that the raven would have experienced a terrific shock at being shot out of the sky, and birds often die from the effects of shock alone. This bird, however, gave me the impression of inner strength, and I noticed that on one of its legs it wore a silver ring engraved not with a name and address, as expected, but with what seemed like runic characters which I didn't understand.

The raven seemed alert yet at rest during the remainder of the evening and appeared comfortable in front of the fire. Toby Jug was obviously concerned at the bird's presence in the cottage and stayed very close to me, manoeuvring himself so that I was between him and the raven at all times. We left the raven in the box when Toby and I went up to bed.

Next morning I was first to go down, although Toby Jug had stationed himself at the head of the stairs waiting for me. To my surprise I found the raven perched on the rim of the box where I'd left him and he greeted me with several loud caws, strident sounds in the quiet of the early morning. I thought the bird was male but couldn't be sure since I didn't know how to determine a raven's gender. The creature's appearance was impressive. He looked a majestic bird and his eyes shone with an intelligent gleam. As the morning progressed and I carried out my household chores the raven followed me and, while I was washing the breakfast dishes in the kitchen, flew onto my shoulder, much to the chagrin of Toby Jug who growled and declined to leave the cottage all morning.

'Well now! You have made a quick recovery,' I said to the bird. He cawed and flapped his wings in reply, making me realize all the more that this bird had been trained to live in a house with someone. I found this highly unusual until I remembered that I had done something similar with Toby Jug.

I recalled that in some versions of the biblical story of Noah and the Ark it was a raven that was first released. The birds figured prominently in the mythology of Asia and northern Europe, where the Vikings regarded them as messengers attending the god Odin. In my early school history lessons I had also been told a romantic legend that England would never fall to a foreign invader as long as there were ravens resident at the Tower of London, so a flock is still kept within its precincts.

All at once the raven flew down from my shoulder and commenced drinking from the cold water tap, which I had turned on to clear the sink of washing-up suds. This made me think that he must be hungry as well as thirsty. Quickly I boiled an egg and chopped it up into small pieces, together with some breakfast oats. I presented him with this and true to his kind the raven ate ravenously.

Toby Jug, having stared all the while in disapproval from the kitchen doorway, could tolerate no more and spat and growled. Fearful that he might attack the raven in a fit of jealousy, I let him out. When the raven finished his meal I decided to take him into the garden to see if he had recovered sufficiently to fly home. Not a bit of it. He hopped around on the lawn, pecking deeply into the turf in crow fashion as if to tell me that he was quite content to stay a while longer.

The rest of the day was spent with all three of us 'gardening': me digging over the redundant vegetable patch, the raven following behind me pecking up grubs and worms, and Toby Jug venting his spleen over the raven's presence at any bird which dared to perch in his apple tree. When it was time to quit, I sat resting on my favourite wooden garden seat with a glass of Burgundy, a jealous cat on my knee and a raven roosting on the back of my chair.

'Stop fretting,' I said to Toby Jug. 'It was you who found the bird and alerted me to its presence. I'm not going to adopt it but I do need to look after it until I can discover to whom it belongs. So stop sulking!' I am convinced he got the gist of my words.

The raven had adopted me as a friend but I felt obliged to pin a notice about him in the window of the village post office so that a bereft owner might retrieve a lost pet. I did not have to wait long. Two days had passed since I had put up the notice and I was again working in the garden accompanied by a possessive cat and a tame raven when a strange woman appeared, standing by the garage. I hadn't heard or seen her arrive – she was just suddenly there. Startled by her abrupt appearance, I stared towards her.

'I believe you have my raven. He's called Kutkh after the raven god.' The name sounded like 'Kukk' and I only found out later how it was spelled. At the sound of his name the raven, which had been busily engaged in foraging, looked up and flew to the woman's shoulder. It proceeded to rub itself against her face as she kissed and petted him, leaving no doubt that the bird was hers.

'He's my mentor and familiar,' she said. 'And my name is Melissa. I am known as the Witch of Rampton Hall.' She held out a long-fingered, bony hand in greeting, which I shook in mine.

'I see that you keep a black cat,' she said.

'Yes, actually he's black and white but mainly black, and he's called Toby Jug. He found your raven in distress in the garden after it had been shot and summoned me.'

'Bless you both,' she said. 'I've been distraught since he went missing and I am so relieved to find him. I thought he might have been killed. Gamekeepers shoot at large wild birds all the time. Please come to visit us at the Hall. Saturday would suit me, and bring your cat. I'd like to celebrate Kutkh's return with you,' she added.

In all politeness I felt I had to agree to call, but I had an uneasy feeling in her presence and I wasn't at all sure that Toby and I should visit. There was something strange about her and her raven, and I didn't warm to the idea of visiting a person associated with witchcraft. I asked about her in the village and learned that the general swell of opinion was to keep well away from Rampton Hall. This left me in a quandary, which I hadn't resolved when on the Friday morning I received a shock through the post.

It was a 'Dear John' letter from my girlfriend Maddy in the USA, who was still on secondment from Alnwick College to a university in Rhode Island. Apparently she had fallen in love with a man called Brad, to whom she had become engaged, and would not be returning to England. It was an emotional blow that I hadn't expected, even though we were little more than good friends and not engaged. The impact of her letter made me feel lonely and rejected, so that by the time Saturday came I didn't give a fig about the wisdom or otherwise of visiting the Witch of Rampton Hall.

I set out expecting the worst and had taken time to tell Toby Jug to be ready to make a quick exit. Whether he understood me or not, I knew that he would take his cue from me. As we set out on the journey of just a couple of miles down the A1 my mood was strained. Rampton Hall was a compact, Gothic building. It presented a weird aspect even in the sunshine and I thought it must look spectral in the darkness. As we arrived, the lady came out to meet the car but there was no sign of her raven. She showed me around the outside of the Hall where there were a number of dilapidated buildings in stone and, more interestingly, a large pond upon which a family of ducks was busy feeding.

'One of my ancestors was bound and gagged and then

thrown in there because she was accused of witchcraft. It was the late seventeenth century and there was great fear of witches at that time.'

'What happened?' I asked.

'She floated instead of sinking and this was taken as a sure sign that she was a witch. She was dragged from the pond and taken before the Witchfinder's Court where she pleaded for a second chance, which was granted, and she was pardoned. But she had the power and she cured a sick child who was possessed by an evil spirit and on another occasion demonstrated her goodness by turning sour milk pure. She barely escaped being burned at the stake.'

'But was she a witch?' I asked, having become interested by her story. She laughed at my question.

'Of course she was. All the first-born women in our family inherited the gift of second sight and the power of the occult.'

'What happened to her?'

'She died in bed of "natural causes" after marrying and having four daughters, lucky woman. Come and have something to eat and bring your cat from the car.'

I retrieved Toby from the car and let him follow behind me as I walked through the ancient wooden door into the Hall. It led to a winding, wood-panelled corridor and into a small room with stone walls and tall stained-glass windows which cast a diffused, coloured glow into the room. A side table had been set with two wooden chairs. Several elegant food dishes had been set out and at the sight of them I suddenly felt hungry. My host, who was already seated, waved me to the chair opposite.

'I hope you like vegetarian food?'

I nodded as she served me a plate of hot wild black rice with green lentils and a covering of fresh coriander. The meal tasted delicious.

'I collect all my food locally, some from the farmers' market and some from the woods and hedgerows.'

I noticed Toby Jug was feeding from a dish of food on the floor.

'Your cat is eating braised leveret. I did not kill it. I don't hurt wildlife, they are all my friends. It was found strangled by a farmer's fence only this morning as I collected wild herbs. I thought your cat, being a carnivore by nature, would appreciate the meat.'

'It certainly looks that way,' I said as I noticed Toby not only eating heartily but wagging his tail at the same time. I then thanked her for her consideration and efforts on our behalf. She inclined her head in acknowledgement of the compliment.

'You are most welcome,' she said. 'After all, I am obliged to you for saving my raven.'

'Where did you get him?' I asked.

'A farmer's wife I had helped recover from a fever brought him to me. She had found him as a fledgling under a bush where he had fallen after some hooligan men had shot his parents and destroyed the nest. The other nestlings had been strangled.'

'How disgusting!' burst from me.

'Surely you are aware that many people take pleasure in hunting and killing wildlife. Many country folks fear and hate ravens because of their links to black magic.'

I decided that, witch or not, I really liked her.

A loud cawing from the roof above the room signalled that Kutkh had returned from whatever he'd been doing. Melissa rose quickly, and her long gypsy-style dress made swishing sounds as she hastened outside.

'Come and see what Kutkh has brought you!' she called.

With mounting curiosity I joined her outside. She was stroking and petting her raven, which was perched on a flat stone topping a wall. In front of the bird lay a single white egg with a bluish hue.

'Kutkh has brought you an egg from a wood pigeon's nest. Don't worry about the pigeon's loss because they have multiple broods.'

'I'm totally mystified, Melissa. Why an egg?'

'I asked him to retrieve the egg without breaking it for you. He carried it in his beak. Isn't he clever?'

'He most certainly is!'

'Tonight you must lay this egg by your bed and in the morning cook and eat it. All your recent sorrows will be banished from your heart, never to return.'

'But how did you know?' I hadn't mentioned anything about Maddy.

'I know things about people. I'm a witch.'

I glanced across at Melissa and smiled my thanks, and then I turned towards her raven. We looked each other straight in the eye and without the least trace of embarrassment I thanked the bird for his gift.

I stared across at her as she sorted the dinner plates and I saw a woman of middle age who looked fit and well with a fresh-faced countenance slightly tanned by time spent outdoors. She had bright blue eyes and a piercing gaze when she looked directly at you, which was her habit when speaking. She left the room briefly, which gave me the opportunity to study some photographs adorning the walls. I only had time to view an assortment of matronly-looking women, lookalikes of her, before she returned with two dessert bowls. I tasted a spoonful and it was exquisite. She told me it was made of honey from apple and greengage blossom with preserved bilberries and rosehips in a kind of elderflower liquor. The dessert was coated in clotted cream with a sprinkling of almonds and elegantly adorned with a layer of buttercup petals. I leaned back contentedly in my chair and stroked Toby Jug, who had jumped on my knee, as I asked her, 'Where is Kutkh?'

She smiled enigmatically. 'He's on a mission to bring another present for you.'

'What might that be?' I asked in some surprise.

'Wait and see,' she replied, her eyes twinkling. At that moment there came a loud cawing.

'Kutkh has returned and look what he has brought you.' She went outside.

The sight that met me as I caught up with her was the raven standing in front of a sprig with a white berry on it that looked remarkably like mistletoe.

'He has brought you a sprig from a sacred bush known only to us, which will bring you good fortune in love.'

'Well, I'm most grateful for the presents, but why?'

'A wood pigeon embodies the mystical spirits of the woods. Its song is the voice of the tree spirits to bring calm and peace to all things when they hear the balm of its cooing. The mistletoe berry is a love token. That's why.'

I thanked Melissa and the raven for my presents and promised to do as she advised. Melissa beamed and the raven fluffed his jet-black feathers as if also to signal approval.

'Before you go I want to show you and your cat something.' Without another word she walked back inside the Hall. I followed with Toby Jug at my heels. She led us into a large room which was flagged with stone paving covering the entire floor. She stopped by a massive floorstone with an iron rung set in its front end.

'I need a favour from you. According to an old deed there are tunnels beneath here from which disturbing sounds echo all over the Hall, especially at night. I cannot investigate this alone as I need help to lift this heavy stone. Cats are psychically empowered to recognize occult forces, which makes you and your cat ideal to find out whatever lies beneath this place.'

I looked at Toby, who gave me one of his enigmatic stares as if he realized that there was something unusual about all this. For my part I just thought of the saying, 'There's no such thing as a free lunch.'

Oh well, I didn't mind helping the lady. I leaned down and put my hand through the iron rung, but my attempt to lift the stone failed.

'It will require a block and tackle to shift this weight,' I said. 'I'll need to see what I can organize and come back another day.'

'I would greatly appreciate your help. You and your cat

are heaven sent for this purpose. It's as if Kutkh's accident and your rescue of him were ordained.'

'I'm not so sure about that,' I said cynically. 'But I will do what I can to help and I must admit my curiosity has been aroused. Whether Toby Jug will go down there when we open it is another matter, since he tends to scare easily.'

'I'm sure you will both do your best. Anyway I have no one else I can trust.'

After saying goodbye, Toby and I left for home. In my mind I was not at all sure what to make of it all but I did place the wood pigeon's egg on a saucer at my bedside together with the sprig. After a while, I decided to go ahead with the venture. At the very least it would prove an interesting exploration like something out of a John Buchan story. I was sure that I could borrow some gear from the local garage and return next weekend to lift that stone, even though a new term at college was about to start and I had much to do beforehand. I watched Toby Jug foraging around the garden looking for one of his red balls and wondered how he would react to going down into a dungeon.

The new academic year at Alnwick College is always a busy time with female students, many of whom had never been away from home before, settling in to live in the medieval buildings of the castle. It was always deemed best to begin academic classes as soon as possible to offset the factor of homesickness, so I was busy throughout the week with both teaching and admin. By the time Saturday morning came around again I was ready to do something different for a change.

Having carried out household chores at the cottage, it was midmorning before I could call at the garage to borrow the pulleys and chains needed to hoist the stone trap door. As I drove up to Rampton Hall, I passed Melissa out foraging along the hedgerows. She waved a greeting and followed me to the Hall.

I parked as near as I could to the entrance and Melissa helped me to carry the gear into the stone-floored room. First of all, I used a pair of steps to loop a rope over the rafter in the wooden ceiling and hang the pulleys above the stone trap door. Then I adjusted the chains, fixed a hook into the iron rung and hauled away. The trap door gave a tremendous screech and then slowly began to lift.

I looked around for Toby Jug, who had vanished at the first screech, and saw that he'd jumped onto one of the narrow ledges of the long windows. At least he hadn't run back to the car. As I pulled on the chains again the stone door was hoisted upright and I jammed it open with a thick wooden baton. I peered down into the cavity below and saw stone steps leading downwards. Melissa produced a large oil lantern to supplement a battery torch I had brought with me, and we carefully began to descend.

I led the way with Melissa behind me holding the lantern aloft with a long wooden pole. There were fourteen steps down to a passage, which gave access to a tunnel. I stopped at the bottom of the steps and looked back up to the entrance. There, framed in the opening, was Toby Jug. He seemed to be dithering about whether to follow me or not, but curiosity – or was it attachment? – won in the end and he swiftly joined me. Melissa lost no time in striding ahead, lantern held aloft to carve a swathe of light through the darkness of the tunnel. We turned a corner to be confronted by a stout wooden door, which opened at a forceful push from both of us. We stepped into a wide room and saw a shape against the far wall.

'What is that? Is it an altar?' Melissa asked, pointing to what seemed to be some kind of raised platform built into the wall. She strode forward and placed the oil lamp on the platform.

'Look at this!' she exclaimed, pointing towards the centre of the altar. The object was a small skull that looked as if it had belonged to a child. Near it was a pile of bones already decayed and powdery.

'It looks like a sacrificial offering of some kind,' I said. 'And there seems to be an inscription written on the wall.'

Shining my torch on it, I could just read the old-fashioned script:

HEED WELL THE TRUTH HERE REVEALED
TIME IS AN ILLUSION
NEITHER WAS THERE A BEGINNING
NOR WILL THERE BE AN END
ONLY AN INFINITY OF THE PRESENT

As the words sunk in, they stirred a memory of a philosophy lecture at university but I struggled to identify their origin. There was no indication of who had written the inscription on the wall, but I could see from the expression on her face that it had deeply affected Melissa. She began examining the remains of the child when she uttered a sharp exclamation of horror. In the dim light of the dungeon she seemed to be holding something small that looked like animal hide covered in fur.

'What is it?' I asked, beginning to feel spooked.

'Not now. I'll tell you later.'

Just then Toby Jug startled me by suddenly jumping up to scramble onto my shoulder, his usual position at times of danger or anxiety. He then began to wail in my ear. Perhaps he had sensed what Melissa was holding in her hand.

As if to change the subject, Melissa looked across at me and pointed to a door in the corner of the wall by the altar. Without a word further she abruptly moved away and began pushing at the door. I felt obliged to help and our combined efforts succeeded in opening the door into another room that was packed out with an odd assortment of objects. When we took a closer look, we were both horrified. It seemed that we had found an ancient torture chamber. In the glare of the lantern we viewed a hideous collection of instruments.

Toby Jug was still clinging on as if his life depended on it and still uttering wails that were beginning to fray my nerves. I told him firmly to 'Shut up!', as his cries were disturbing in that gruesome place. Melissa looked across at me and I could see by her facial expression in the yellow glare of the lantern that she was on edge.

'This is why I wanted you to bring your cat. This is a bad place and he knows why.'

I looked around and could not but agree. There were beds of nails, chairs with spikes on the seats and backs, and chains with manacles for imprisoning victims. There were ugly-looking curved knives and hatchets laid out on a table as if for an operation of a macabre nature. An array of swords and axes was leant against one of the walls, but most frightening of all were the images of ghouls and devils painted on the wall. One of the most horrific pictures was of a standing, human-like figure covered in fur with a fierce-looking animal's head. The disturbing and sinister thing about the figure was its feral, yellow eyes, with tints of red around the edges. The eyes seemed to be looking directly at us and, as we moved, they appeared to follow us.

'A werewolf!' Melissa gasped, looking at the image.

I turned to her and said, 'I've had enough of this place. I'm leaving now.' Without another word, we headed back to the stone steps.

As we approached the stairs, a disembodied voice broke into song.

It was terrifying.

'That must be the girl whose bones we found. She's singing to us now to have her spirit released,' said Melissa.

This settled the matter for me. I resolved never to enter that place again. Toby Jug had been quite right to wail and I was sorry I yelled at him. The song had such a melancholy ring to it and was so full of anguish that it made me feel like crying. I took Toby Jug from my shoulder and hugged him in my arms without saying a word. This was too much for me and I bolted up the rest of the stairs.

We relaxed with relief over sandwiches and coffee prepared by Melissa. Toby Jug, who was much relieved to be back in a normal setting, had a dish of rabbit livers cooked in catmint with meaty gravy, which added to his sense of restored wellbeing. She had bought the rabbit meat at the farmer's market specially for Toby Jug, even though she herself never ate meat.

I told Melissa that the torture chamber bore a remarkable resemblance to one I had seen at Sir Humphry Wakefield's castle at Chillingham, but this dungeon was much more gruesome.

Melissa then told me about the historical rise of the occult in Northumberland. 'Old beliefs and customs were criminalized, so folk developed secret practices that resulted in macabre occult customs. Demon worship produced monsters, vampires and werewolves which preyed on the innocent. I believe that these practices changed the physical make-up of some people, occasioning a return to prehistoric primitive manifestations.' Here she paused for breath and stared out of the window towards the distant trees.

'What I picked up from that bench was a piece of animal skin with fur on it. I think it came from the young skeleton that was there and probably was an example of a ritual sacrifice of a human who was a shape-shifter – a human being who could for a brief period change into an animal and back again. It had probably been captured in animal form and ritually executed. The lifelike picture of the werewolf in the torture chamber confirmed my suspicions.'

'Yes,' I said, 'The eyes of that creature were very lifelike but deeply dark, which I found most alarming.'

'You would find it more disturbing to meet one on a moonlit walk in the countryside!'

'Do you really believe such beasts exist?'

'Yes, in rare circumstances. Humans adapt to the exigencies of the moment with survival in mind.'

'Well, I don't. I think it is all an overblown myth used by religion to frighten people, especially children. Like the Little Red Riding Hood fairy tale.'

'Have it your own way, Denis, but I have been close to the dark side of nature and seen things I fear with my own eyes. If you believe that living creatures have a spirit which lives on after they die, then it is easy to accept that there are ghosts which haunt places.'

'I agree with you there because people I respect tell me of ghosts that haunt Alnwick Castle, but I don't believe they can do us any harm. That torture chamber is just an example of how inhumane some people were to other people. My suggestion is that we close that access and never open it again. It could disturb somebody's mind if they witnessed what we saw. After all, it nearly drove my cat crazy. He was very frightened. I have never seen him so scared.'

'Well, you know what I said when I asked you to bring your cat with you. Cats, like ravens, are in tune with the spirit world more so than we are. Your cat gave us an early warning of bad vibrations when he jumped on your shoulder and started wailing. He was alerting you to a presence we couldn't see but he could. It was an omen.'

Melissa gave me a hard stare. Then she nodded and said, 'You're right about sealing it up. Let's do that, but before we close the trap door I'd like to place a wreath of angelica and some other herbs to bless and make peace with any spirits down there, especially whoever was singing. There will no doubt be others in that damned place who are striving to be set free. I will do my utmost to bring them the blessings they need, but that need not concern you.'

'Fair enough,' I said. 'I'll wait around until you're done then I'll help you shut it all off.'

After she carried out her blessing ritual I closed the stone trapdoor and took all the pulleys and chains back to the car to return them to the garage the next day.

Strangely, it was only when I came across Maddy's letter again later in the week that I realized that I hadn't thought about her at all. I remembered Melissa's words and her 'egg spell' – perhaps the spell had worked its magic, just as she said it would.

I treated that Saturday experience at Rampton Hall as a closed book. I didn't want to think about it ever again, but I did accept an invitation from Melissa to attend a barbecue at the Hall. I didn't bring Toby Jug because he really didn't like the Hall. This was just as well, because after a friendly social gathering of local folk and a tasty meal of pork chops and one of Melissa's herbal salads, I found that when I came to leave, my car would not start.

Feeling quite replete after the food and wine, I decided to walk the few miles home rather than bother with a taxi. Although the main road had little traffic at that time of night, I decided to take a short cut across the fields, following paths I knew well that meandered past Willowbrook Farm and skirted the edge of Stag Wood.

Strange indeed is the working of the mind. As I passed

by a woodland copse of mature trees I registered the distinct impression that I was being stalked. Even shadows cast by a three-quarter moon can play tricks with the imagination, but I swear a dark figure was keeping pace with me as I walked alongside a line of trees. It was then that memories of Melissa's tales of werewolves and shape-shifters invaded my mind and I began to hurry. By the time I reached the minor country road leading to Felton I was almost running.

I stopped for a moment to calm myself and catch my breath, but it was then that I heard the howling. I convinced myself that it was only a big dog baying at the moon in a backyard somewhere, but nevertheless I could swear that it was a wolf I had heard and it made me shiver. I'd never had any superstitious fear of wolves or werewolves before, but I started to wonder just what our intrusion into the dungeon had unleashed.

I was relieved at last to see the cottage nestling in peaceful tranquillity. Once inside with Toby Jug on my knee and a glass of single-malt whisky in hand, I reflected on my fear that night. Wise little Toby Jug had been right to never want to go near Rampton Hall again. It was then that I made up my mind to have nothing more to do with the Hall, Melissa, her raven or the witchcraft stories. As soon as I had decided this, Toby Jug began to purr loudly.

I was glad to be in my home with my ever faithful cat companion. I determined to give him heaps of tender loving care over the next few days to make up for the stress I'd put him through of late.

In the afternoon of the next day I boarded the bus for

Eshott village and walked the paths to Rampton Hall to pick up my car. I'd brought battery extension leads with me in case I needed help in starting the engine, but the really eerie link to the experience of the previous night was that the car started first time. It made me wonder if the spirits there were playing a gruesome game with me. Just to be sure, I had the local garage check the battery. They found nothing wrong with it.

TOBY, FYNN AND THE OTTER HUNT

S oon I was once again deeply involved in work at the college during the autumn term. Many of my most interesting work adventures occurred outside the college walls in the autumn and summer terms, when I would head out on trips to supervise students on teaching practice in remote areas of Northumberland and some-times out as far as Selkirk and Galashiels in Scotland.

The major drawback was that I usually could not take Toby Jug with me so he had to stay at my mother's house. Neither of us liked this enforced separation and it was always grand to be back together in the cottage again. At the time, I was still studying part time for my Master of Education, so I was at home working in the cottage most evenings, which suited Toby Jug as he would have me to himself. He would lie next to my typewriter, purring hap-pily away as I recorded my research analysis. The garden also continued to take up a great deal of my free time, harvesting the vegetables I'd planted in the early spring in addition to weeding and collecting piles of leaves that had already started falling with the advent of autumn winds.

One evening when I'd stayed late at my desk in the college, I made my customary call to the White Swan on my way home. I ordered a glass of wine and a plate of ham sandwiches and, as I relaxed in front of the coal fire, I noticed a sign which sent my blood pressure soaring. It announced a meeting of the Northumbrian Otter Hunt Club scheduled for the following Wednesday at 7.30 p.m. in the hotel's main lounge. I was furious that these magnificent creatures were being pursued for the pleasure of a bloodthirsty minority, so I determined to attend the meeting and assert my views.

As I leafed through the bar's copy of the *Northumberland Gazette*, I was further incensed by a photograph of the otter hunt's leader, a stocky woman of middle years wearing waders up to her thighs and a floppy sun hat, carrying a stout stick and surrounded by a pack of hounds. I had often thought of having an otter as a pet, since I had heard what affectionate animals they are. The next day I penned a passionate letter to the editor of the *Gazette* condemning the practice of otter hunting and calling for its abolition on humanitarian grounds. The published letter would cause me trouble later.

At the appointed time I was present in the lounge of the White Swan. The chairman, a local member of the nobility, called the packed meeting to order at the appointed time and commenced thanking local farmers and salmon fishermen for their wholehearted support for the hunt. This was accompanied by a series of loud clapping as each supporter's name was called out. A plate was then passed around for donations for the hunt. When it came to me, my vociferous refusal drew a host of hostile stares.

Then the chairman continued the meeting by praising a member for successfully 'blooding' three young hounds. On asking exactly what 'blooding' entailed, I was told that otter bodies were fed to the hounds to familiarize them with the scent and taste of the animals. When I interrupted the speaker to ask whether the otters fed to the hounds were alive or dead, a huge gentleman, sporting a large ginger moustache, barked the answer 'They're only pups, stupid!' which raised a laugh at my expense.

I took a long look at this man and I didn't like what I saw. The corpulent, overfed and over-indulged body was offensive enough but, worst of all, I saw with mounting horror that he was wearing a small, white bone tiepin. This, I knew, was a trophy otter hunters boasted about: the bone from the genitalia of the male otter, the boar. I felt sick in the pit of my stomach at the sight of it.

Who were these people – throwbacks to an earlier age when brutality was a signifier of a 'real man'? As I struggled to control the sickening rage within me, I heard all around me enthusing about the blooding and the hunt.

There then followed a long monologue by the chairman explaining, for my benefit, the code of practice in the countryside to keep order, protect fish stocks and control ferocious wildlife that threatened farm animals, the poultry business and pheasant rearing. Just as I counterattacked these arguments, a policeman entered the meeting and escorted me outside to loud jeers and applause from the members. I was cautioned and told to go home or I would be arrested and charged with disturbing the peace. The hotel receptionist later told me that someone in the meeting had identified me as a troublemaker and asked the hotel to call the police in case I became violent.

It appalled me to think of otters being killed for sport. I had seen otter families cavorting freely along the banks of the Coquet many times when I was out riding, and it always gave my heart a lift to watch them as they dived for fish and played wrestling games with each other. I talked it over with Toby Jug, who had lost his mother, his brother and nearly his own life as a result of the hunter's cruel mentality. He was accustomed to my speeches on the various issues that troubled me. He would sit on my knee during the harangue and look for all the world as if he understood every word. Then he would purr loudly and lick the back of my hand to show he understood and agreed with me. Of course, I sussed out that he was mostly just responding to the attention I was lavishing upon him, but he was doing me a worthwhile service in helping me to articulate my arguments. Following my rant to Toby Jug, I formed the nucleus of an idea for a course of action on behalf of the otters. First, I needed an ally to make my project possible, and I knew the ideal person to ask.

As the sun was setting over the fields and woodlands of Felton village I set out alone. It was dusk when I found the cottage where Tom lived. At first it seemed that no one was in, as my knocks on the door produced no response, but then suddenly he was standing next to me.

Tom lived on the cusp of the law and he explained that

when he'd heard my knock he'd slipped out the back in case it was someone he didn't wish to meet. Such caution was second nature for Tom who, was almost as feral as the creatures he lived alongside. He was so secretive and withdrawn by nature that he didn't invite me into his run-down cottage but directed me to sit on a stump outside his front door. He squatted beside me as I outlined my plan.

I asked him if he could supply a substance that would mask the scent of otters so that the hounds would not be able to find their trail. To my delight, Tom became quite animated at my request. The wild animals that shared his domain were his fellow travellers and he was staunchly possessive about them. His eyes lit up at the prospect of thwarting the authorities, and his whippet, Pitch, gave a muted growl to show accord with his master's enthusiasm. Tom, a man of few words, not only promised to provide what I asked for but volunteered to help the whole enterprise.

'They drive stakes in the entrances of the otter holts below the water line so as to cut off escape and they dig the pups out of their den so they can be caught easy. If you like I can see to it that the otters aren't barred from their holts.'

I thanked Tom and marvelled at the speech I'd just heard from a normally reticent man. I told him the hunt was arranged for the following Saturday near the end of September and I'd need the 'mixture' the Friday before so that I could carry out my plan. I left Tom and his black whippet to the peace of the darkening forest and headed by car for Alnwick.

My next port of call was Isabelle White's stables at Windy Edge. I asked her if I could hire one of her horses to ride along the river from the Castle Pastures down to Lesbury Bridge on the Friday I had earmarked for my mission.

'You could have Fynn if you're not going on too long a trek. Diane Forester has given up riding her and she's still a reliable mount.' I was delighted with her suggestion, as a very young Toby Jug and I had enjoyed a great adventure with Fynn one summer. I arranged to pick up the horse around three o'clock in the afternoon, which would give me ample time for what I had in mind. I thanked Isabelle but didn't mention anything about my mission. As far as she knew I just wanted a recreational ride out.

I drove home feeling well satisfied. I told Toby that we'd be back together with Fynn soon, and he could sit with me on the horse's back or follow us on foot, since I'd be frequently dismounting to apply the substance Tom was preparing for me.

Late on Thursday there was a furtive knock at the conservatory door. Tom and his dog usually came and went like phantoms, but sharp-eared Toby had already alerted me to the sound of them coming to call. Tom presented me with a hessian sack about a third full with some substance. Again, this usually reticent man was full of information. He was anxious to tell me that the hunt club had been out with their spades digging holes in the otter holts.

'I loosened the stakes they put down so the otters can get passed them but not so it shows. The stuff in the bag will spoil the hounds' scent. They'll not be any use at sniffing trails for at least a week,' he said with relish. 'Don't let your cat near it cos it might make him sick. My dog will have naught to do with it.' This statement was accompanied by a rare smile that lit up his normally morose face.

I thanked Tom and offered him some money to cover his expenses but he would accept none.

'It was a pleasure to help,' he said, and with that he was gone, lost in the darkness of the garden.

On Friday I hurried through my work at the college and left early. The weather was dry with hazy sunshine down by the river. I was becoming increasingly excited at the prospect of denying the otter hunt a killing.

Toby Jug appeared to share my excitement as he leapt onto the front seat of the car before I'd even shut the cottage back door. He became even more elated when he saw me saddling Fynn. I had become extremely fond of Fynn when we went for a camping trip in the Cheviot foothills, and I was pleased to find that she seemed to remember me. She certainly remembered Toby Jug and it was a joy to see them sniffing each other to renew their acquaintance again. I thanked Maureen, the stable girl on duty, and with the hessian sack tied onto the back of the saddle, everything was ready for the operation.

It felt good to be on Fynn's back once more as I rode down the hill from the stables with Toby Jug perched on the saddle in front of me. As we neared the river the sun was still high in the sky and there was a pleasant breeze fanning our faces. The river was running fast as I dismounted by the huge slabs of stepping stones that forded the water below the weir.

This was an ideal location to begin smearing the concoction Tom had given me. I had seen otters here before as they fished for salmon waiting to jump the weir. As I worked my way around the stones and the banks, smearing on liberal amounts of the substance with a trowel and gloved hands, Toby was content simply to snooze on the saddle while Fynn took advantage of the opportunity to graze on the lush meadow grass at the water's edge.

Then we were off, moving down river, stopping here and there to deposit the mixture that I hoped would do the trick the next day. I noted the trees we passed on our way – huge, towering monoliths planted in ages long past and just now reaching maturity. When I reached Lesbury, Toby Jug went on a foray of his own under the old stone bridge, sniffing around the ledges and arches. Perhaps he could detect the presence of otters, but he shied away from the places I had coated with the mixture. Then we were back on track, this time working the other side of the river as we headed back to the starting point.

For a while Toby preferred to scout his own course by the river, studiously ignoring my ministrations but investigating suspicious-looking holes and wide crevices in the mature trees. Where there were flattened boulders on the river bed where otters could rest and where they undoubtedly would leave their scent, I dismounted, sometimes standing in the river, and smeared the paste across the stone's surface. We halted at the point where the river had meandered around and formed a miniature ox-bow. Looking down from the saddle, I could see the dark forms of young trout poised near the surface in the evening sunlight. It seemed a convenient stopping place so I dismounted to take a break.

I loosened Fynn's saddle girth and fed her some apple and carrot treats. Toby Jug had a portion of chicken and I had a ham-and-onion sandwich washed down with a glass of Châteauneuf-du-Pape poured from a hip flask. This was part of my ongoing philosophy of trying to enjoy life whatever the circumstances. A great many people, I thought, including many of my work colleagues, would gladly change their mundane surroundings and swap places with me at this moment if they only knew. It was a delightful evening and I raised my wine glass in salutation to the winsome charms of the countryside stretched out around me.

Ready once more for the ride, I checked Fynn's saddle girth and, whilst Toby Jug was scampering about chasing flies in the grass, I was just wrapping my wine glass in a hand towel when a red-faced farmer appeared abruptly and angrily accused me of illegally fishing the river. A brief altercation ensued in which I protested my innocence of any poaching and asserted my right to ride along the banks of the River Coquet. I rode off and left him bellowing in the wind. Toby had begun to tire and leapt onto the saddle to have a rest. Also, he didn't respond well to noisy people like the farmer. The rest of the ride was uneventful and I simply enjoyed listening to the calls of the wildlife around me as the animals awakened with the dusk. I heard the bark of a fox from the depths of Denwick Woods and later the scream of a rabbit, probably the victim of some weasels. A kestrel, red feathers catching the setting sun, hovered over a drainage ditch as it hunted voles.

On nearing the hill leading up to Windy Edge Farm, the sun was dropping towards the horizon. I looked back from the top of the hill and saw a flight of mallards splashing down to spend the night on the weir. This was the Northumberland I loved, this was my country. As wisdom has it: what you love needs to be protected and cherished or you will lose it. This was precisely why I had done what I had done. Meanwhile, Toby was having a quick catnap snooze whilst clinging on to my shoulder. At the stables I unsaddled Fynn, fed her some grain and told her what a wonderful horse she was while the two teenage girls manning the stables petted and fussed over Toby Jug.

I was glad to return to the cottage and rest, listening to a composition by Delius entitled 'A walk in the paradise garden'. The music soothed my cat and me, and I thanked Toby Jug for helping me on the ride. This cat of mine cared about me in ways that people never had, and I loved and respected him above all else. Afterwards we shared some of the cold game pie a kind neighbour had left me for supper and we retired to bed in the hope that my efforts would not have been in vain. Tomorrow, when the hunt sallied forth, there would hopefully be no otters to be found.

In the morning I cooked a good old English breakfast of fresh eggs and home-cured bacon bought from the farmers' market in Alnwick, grilled venison sausages, black pudding and slices of crunchy fried bread. Toby Jug was more than pleased with his share of the sausages. Later we relaxed in the warm morning sun, and from the garden seat fronting the outside of the conservatory I basked in the birdsong coming from the trees. I could hear a song thrush whistling a lavish repertoire of trills and whistles to impress his mate. He was imitating other birdcalls he'd heard to supplement his own range. Somewhere above my head a blackbird was warbling a tune in praise of the morning. I was in my element.

Toby Jug then took up his favourite haunt in the old apple tree, from which he could survey the comings and goings of the village. I noticed a bounty of cooking apples on the branches of the tree, which would make tasty apple pies when baked.

Towards midmorning a neighbour poked his head over my fence with the news that there had been ructions going on in the Duke's pastures this morning due to the otter hunt being sabotaged. Someone had put down a poison that had made the hounds sick. Apparently they were retching and vomiting all over the place and the vet had to be called. The police had been advised and the Duke had offered a reward for information.

'Serves them right for persecuting innocent animals,' I said.

'Well, there's many folks up in arms about it cos otters are taking salmon and sea trout from the river.'

'How else can they survive?' I almost shouted. 'Anyway, I couldn't care less,' I said, aware that I was being rather rude.

'Well, some people are always making trouble,' he said, and disappeared from view.

'And so are nosey parkers!' I called after him. I felt a warm glow of satisfaction as I revelled in the news. The otters would survive to live another day.

I felt sorry for the hounds, but at least they would recover, whereas the otters would not have survived the hunt.

Alnwick was an old-fashioned town with a feudal lord in the form of the Duke of Northumberland ruling the roost. He was Grand Master of the Percy Fox Hunt and an ardent protagonist of the hunting-shooting fraternity, as his noble ancestors had been from time immemorial.

'The times they are a-changing,' I said to myself. Toby Jug, from his perch among the apples, gave me a look of full assent.

In the weeks that followed I was totally occupied with college matters. The little spare time I had in the evenings was spent reading and writing for my degree. As summer nights gave way to the shortening of daylight, I would often sit late at night with just the light from a single candle to illuminate the room. I'd draw back the curtains and gaze out onto the rose garden in the soft starlight. Toby Jug liked to share such quiet interludes with me by lying across my neck and shoulders like a woollen scarf. Sometimes we would sit together this way in silence, watching a little owl hunting mice in the compost heap and pipistrelle bats flit across our line of sight.

On the dark and cold mornings of autumn I found it required a supreme effort to get to work early, but a refreshing mug of hot sweet tea and a slice of toast spread with honey, plus the friendly presence of Toby Jug, would do wonders to bolster my spirits. I was always keen to return home in the evenings and call for Toby if he wasn't in his usual place to greet me. When I saw his grizzly, furry face again all would be well with the world and we would enter our cottage home as happy as could be. Then it was an easy task to close the curtains, light the log fire and enjoy that first glow of heat with a glass of Burgundy to drink as the cat and I crouched by the hearth. Then to contemplate what delicacies I could cook up for dinner. A dish of chicken livers would suffice for Toby Jug and a plate of steak, leeks and potatoes fried in beef fat would do very nicely for me. Then would be study time, with Toby playing a fast game of red pawball on the floor before lying across some of my papers to indicate his additional interest in matters academic.

One day in the weeks following the otter hunt I had to be in Berwick-upon-Tweed by eight-thirty to introduce some new students to the junior school where they would have their first experience of teaching. I always felt cold in Berwick, whatever the season, perhaps because the buildings of dark grey stone and the high chimneys have a forlorn look about them. I left Toby in the cottage finishing a saucer of warm milk containing a crumpled digestive biscuit and some pieces of steak from my meal of the previous night. He saw me leave from his appointed station in the old apple tree and I felt a pang, but I couldn't take him on this long trip.

I spent a wearisome day with two students in a class of unruly older children. At lunchtime, I skipped the school meal and drove out to walk along the battlement walls while eating a sausage roll. I was late returning to the cottage that evening and regretted that I would have to return to Berwick every day for the rest of the week.

A highlight of the week was a trip the class teacher had organized to the old Town Hall. The children were fascinated by its prison section, where Saturday-night drunks would be manacled to a sloping shelf. However, from the children's point of view the most interesting feature of the building was a toilet specially built for Queen Elizabeth II when she visited the town. The children's drawings, hung on the classroom wall following the trip, aroused great hilarity as many pictured the Queen wearing a crown seated on the toilet. So much for the innocence of childhood.

During the next week, on my way to Alnwick College I stopped at the Running Fox Café to buy a morning paper and overheard two customers saying that the local priest at St Michael's Church had died. This jogged a memory of my visit to Rampton Hall, during which I had explored one of the building's Gothic towers. Melissa had told of a priest hole halfway up a spiral staircase but still challenged me to spot the hidden door. Try as I might, I couldn't find a doorway in any of the oak panels. It was Toby Jug who eventually pinpointed the concealed opening by sniffing suspiciously at one of the cracks in the worn stairs. On investigation I located a gap under the stone just sufficient to insert a hand. When I gripped the stone and pulled upwards, the slab lifted easily and beneath it was an empty cavity wide enough and deep enough to accommodate myself and Toby Jug. Inside the only furnishing was an antique wooden stool with three legs of the sort my grandmother called a 'cracket'. Once I lowered myself down into the hole, closely shadowed by Toby Jug, the stone slab above our heads slid back into place. As I sat in the black darkness the stone trap door above me suddenly opened and there was Melissa smiling down at us.

'I guessed you'd find it,' she said.

'Well actually it was Toby who showed me the handhold,' I replied.

'He's a smart little cat, all right. I've brought you a candle and some matches so you can get a real feel of what it was like to be a Catholic priest in Tudor Times.'

I thanked her, placed the candle on a stone shelf in front of me and lit it before I closed the slab. I wondered if the smoke from the candle might lead to detection, but I realized the staircase was so draughty that the smoke would be wafted away.

After I pushed the slab open again, I asked Melissa, 'Could you see the light of the candle?'

'Negative,' she said, 'but if the priest heard anything he'd put the candle out.'

'Did anyone ever get caught?' I asked.

'Only one I read of, a Jesuit who was burned alive at the stake on the orders of Elizabeth I. The story is that the Priest Hunter used a dog to sniff out lots of priests.'

I said that I would close the slab again to capture more of the feeling of what it must have been like to be a hunted priest.

'Pretty terrifying, I would think,' said Melissa. 'Rather

like being hunted for witchcraft, like my female ancestors. I'll leave you to it, but meet me for some tea before you go.'

I thanked her again, and with the slab closed I meditated on the horrors of Tudor England and the fanaticism that forced people to hide in a tiny stone cell, fearing death simply because of their convictions. Toby Jug, crouching at my feet, mewed at me with such intensity that I got the message that he'd had enough. So had I.

'May God bless the spirit of the poor murdered priest,' I murmured to the stone wall as we made a swift exit from the priest hole. It was the week before my abortive journey into the underground tunnels of the Old Hall. Little did I know what would face me there.

One evening later that week I decided to call into the Northumberland Arms Hotel in Felton for a drink and to catch up on any local news. The hotel lay just down the bank from the cottage and, after feeding Toby Jug, I walked down to the hotel, stopping to look over the bridge and watch the river for a while. As I entered the bar I sensed a change in the normally friendly atmosphere. There were a number of young farmers lounging against the counter and they started rudely commenting among themselves when they noticed me. It transpired that they had read my letter in the *Northumberland Gazette* in opposition to otter hunting and they were in a hostile mood.

One of them turned towards me as I was ordering a drink and said: 'Why don't you f*** off and go back to where you belong?'

I didn't reply as I felt things might easily have got really nasty, so I took my glass of wine and sat down in a far corner of the bar. They continued to mutter among themselves with an occasional belligerent glare in my direction. I quickly finished my drink and left to jeers and catcalls from the assembly.

Much later, as I was busy writing at my desk, I heard a movement outside and a half-brick smashed through my sitting-room window. When I opened the door there was no sign of anyone but I could guess who threw the stone.

My neighbour Laura and her husband came out, having heard the crash of breaking glass. They sympathized with me, saying that it must have been kids, but I knew otherwise. Being attacked in this violent way was shocking, and it was frightening to contemplate what else might happen. I had even more sympathy for those frightened monks hiding in the priest holes.

The sound of the breaking glass had scared Toby out of his wits and he had disappeared. I eventually discovered him upstairs squeezed under a gap between the floor and the bottom of the wardrobe in my bedroom. He was still in a state of shock and he was trembling as I pulled him out. Animals are unable to deal with human violence because they can't understand the reason behind it.

It cost me money to have my window repaired, but I was more determined than ever to continue my campaign against the hunting and killing of otters. To paraphrase William Shakespeare: 'If you prick us do we not bleed? If you poison us do we not die? If you shoot at us and hound us with ferocious beasts are we not terrified beyond toleration?'

Animals cannot plead their case against persecution, but

I can on their behalf. I lament the loss of the bear, the wolf, the beaver and the elk, which have all been eliminated from our shores due to the bloodlust and greed of human kind.

I looked down at my beloved cat on my knee and I thought how much I owed him for his love and companionship – animals are a special gift from nature, not a toy to be discarded at will, and I thought of the other little creatures that I had been glad to befriend in the cottage garden before Toby Jug came into my life.

One of my first garden friends was a robin redbreast. I had seen him following my trail as I dug over the vegetable plot at weekends. It made good sense to him because he was able to feed well on the worms and grubs I uncovered. When I halted digging to take a breather he would remain near me as if he were developing an affection for my company. Occasionally he would perch on the handle of my spade and chirp at me as if to say, 'Thank you.'

Then I started noticing him in the early mornings when I would take my mug of tea into the garden prior to setting off for work. Whilst I drank my tea and extolled the views, this bright little bird would keep flitting around me, chirping away as if expecting me to give him something. Since I rarely ate breakfast on work days I would have nothing to offer him, but I would go inside to get him a few bits of cereal. Sometimes he didn't appear and I worried that he might have been killed by a hawk or a marauding cat, but the next day he would be there as large as life, acting his friendly old self. This bird began to mean something special to me, and soon we developed a close enough friendship for him to take food from my hand.

The scene that welcomed me most mornings as I stood drinking tea would begin at ground level with a slight movement as my feathered friend made his entrance from wherever he pleased. Perhaps it would be from within the dark tangle of hawthorn branches that the radiant figure would hop into sight, or it could be from the green mass of the holly tree, or then again I could find him cheekily waiting on the garden wall in anticipation of my coming. Wherever he was, it warmed my heart to find him there. With silken feathers of cream and rust brown and a breast splashed with crimson, he would greet me with a welcoming chirp. Bright darting eyes would scan my hands for any proffered treats. Confident in his expectation, he would flutter to perch on my wrist and, with beak extended, take morsels of cereal from my open palm. I could feel the faint pulse of his breath brushing my fingers as soft as moonlight. I would raise my mug to drink but he often beat me to it. Alighting on the rim, he would bob and dip to take a token sip of warm tea.

This was to become our habitual morning ritual. Such bold intimacy told of the closeness between soulmates. Together the bird and I would survey the wintry landscape where blizzards had toned the cropped fields with a dusting of white. It was November and winter was showing its hand earlier this year. The outlook from my garden was bleak as Northumberland succumbed to the grip of a glacial frost. Overhead a flock of rooks, black wings against a leaden sky, flew in noisy chorus to their rookery in the pines. As I stood gazing at the scene a ripple of wind fluffed the robin's feathers, driving him to ground, and gave me an icy shiver that hastened me back to the cottage for warmth. Of the robin there would now be no sign, but we meet again on many other mornings. It was a joy to have such contact with a wild bird, but rather than chance or accident, it was something that I felt was meant to be so.

Principal amongst other garden friends was the family of hedgehogs that graced my presence as I sat watching the sunset fade from bands of striped orange and red to a darkening dusk. The coming of night invited these nocturnal wanderers to browse the garden for slugs and snails, good eating in a garden where no pesticides or toxic pellets could poison wildlife. I felt privileged that the sow allowed her three piglets to play a rough-and-tumble game around my feet. For a short time this nightly rendezvous with hedgehogs became a regular occurrence and I made sure that a bowl of warm milk was on offer. It was much appreciated.

It became a night-time habit of mine, despite the chill, to mount a vigil in the darkness to learn what I could of the furtive wildlife inhabiting my garden. Later, if there was moonlight, I might see a flight of bats winging their aerobatics through the trees as they feasted on the swarms of insects buzzing in the foliage. In the morning, many times I would be jarred back to full alertness by the strident calls of the little owls as they hunted through the trees, and I would rise, stiff and tired but jubilant, and then head for bed and leave the night to the real night owls.

The animals of the wild were so important to me, day to day, that the thought of human predators unnecessarily hunting and slaying them for no good reason filled me with disgust. People rarely accused me outright of sabotaging the otter hunt, but my eviction from the hunt meeting and my letter to the *Gazette* made me a prime suspect.

For the remainder of my time at Owl Cottage, and even when I returned to live there again with my wife Catherine years later, there were some locals who still would not forgive me for putting the plight of animals above the sport of humans. However, I always took solace that there was one man, who knew the land and the rivers better than any of them, who shared my views.

Since I had received a further promotion at the college that autumn, I had a little more money available at the end of the month and I decided to put it to good use. I had long desired a domestic freezer, which were becoming more popular with ordinary householders, and made a special trip to Newcastle upon Tyne to buy one. It was delivered the following week and I had it installed in the space freed up at the rear end of the garage. The freezer I chose was a medium-sized chest variety, which would give impetus to my cooking now that I had a place to store pies and fish, which sometimes went to waste through lack of suitable storage space.

As luck would have it, a few days after I had the new freezer installed, Tom and his dog materialized out of the shadows as I was tidying up the leaf-fall outside the patio, ready to go in for the night. His abrupt appearance had me startled, but I tried not to show it as he presented me with a long bundle of something wrapped in newspaper.

'There's something for you and your cat that won't be gracing milord's table tonight.'

'What is it, Tom?' I asked, unwrapping the package and thinking it could be a rabbit or a hare. Instead I found myself holding a gleaming salmon still wet from the river. Its beautiful blue and silver scales shimmered in the half light and it weighed a good four and a half pounds.

'Tom, this is absolutely wonderful, but you shouldn't risk breaking the law for my sake. Would you like to come inside and have something to eat and drink with me?'

'No thank you! I must be about my business, Pitch and me's got ground to cover afore morning so I'll be seeing ye. Don't be worrying yourself about the salmon cos there's plenty more where that come from. Lifted it from right under yon bailiff's nose.' He grinned with relish at the memory of his prowess.

He turned to leave, but halted to face me again.

'That was a reet good thing you done for them otters,' he said with unusual candour.

'It was done from the heart . . .' I began, but he was gone, evaporating into the darkness of the night with his ever faithful dog.

'You'll meet in life with just a few kindred spirits,' my grandmother told me as a boy, 'and when you do you will know them.'

'I reckon I've met one in Tom,' I said to myself as I closed the conservatory door. 'What do you think of that, Toby Jug?' I said, bending down with the package to let him have an appetizing sniff at the salmon. He was, as Jane Austen would have said, 'all amazement'.

Later on, after cutting the fish into steaks, I stored all but two in my new freezer, which had arrived just in the nick of time. I looked out on the garden, now bathed in moonlight, and wished Tom and his dog good hunting as I headed in the direction of the kitchen to cook salmon for our supper.

THE MENACE OF THE
HORNETS' NEST

As the year progressed I was so busy at college and grafting away at my degree studies at home that sometimes life seemed to be just one weary chore after another. Sometimes late at night, with more work yet to complete, I would feel the onset of a dose of self-pity, no doubt helped by listening to Frank Sinatra's album, *Point of No Return*. Then I would look down at the cat on my knee and my mood would lift again.

'Toby Jug, you are all I have to share my life. No woman, no children, nothing except you, pal, but I count myself a lucky guy.' At these words Toby would purr loudly, stretch out his paws, and flex them in pleasure.

The only time during term that I was totally free to do as I pleased was on some weekends, so weather permitting Toby Jug and I would wander the countryside together. It was time to go on a walk again soon, or else we would miss some of the delights of autumn.

We usually ventured on our meanderings in the quiet hours late at night or in the early morning to enjoy the changing seasons. Apart from occasionally encountering

Tom and his dog, we were alone in a world of wild animals and birds. I was especially attracted to the river as it wound its way between the fields and the woodland, sustaining the land and the creatures living there.

Many an early morning before the sun was up my cat and I would stop and stare at the hazy veil hanging over the river, smooth except for ripples of trout breaching the surface in pursuit of flies or a splash as a water vole dived out of the weeds lining the river bank. We were growing to know this landscape like a familiar friend and saw things normally unseen, such as the flattened, bare patch in the grass border of the wheat field where a fox had lain in wait for the rabbits. Nearby, in the thickly wooded copse, between the rotting tree falls there was a hidden gap in the brown earth where a family of badgers had their sett. A pile of rabbit skins lay near the back entrance, which gave access to a stream where the animals drank after dark. Little disturbed the quietude of the broadleaf trees except the drowsy cooing of wood pigeons and the infrequent mooing of the farmer's dairy herd in the adjoining field. Here lies the essence of pastoral England, I remember thinking one spring as Toby and I crossed a cropped hayfield while hares boxed in the half-light.

One particular March night, as I drove away from a country pub where I'd spent the evening with friends, I came upon a tragic sight. The car that had preceded me had hit a buck hare as he crossed the road. I stopped to pick up his body. He was badly injured and just barely alive. I gently laid him on the grass verge at the side of the road, and as I turned to go back to my car I spotted a doe, his mate, watching me. Of course, I thought, hares tend to mate for life. Once inside my car, I saw her in the beam of my headlights lope over to his body and, before I started the engine, I heard the unmistakable whining of her distress as she stood over him.

Toby Jug and I would move along the trails of the wild creatures as we practised our woodcraft. Once, in a hidden spot, we found the remains of a plover's nest plundered by weasels, the broken eggshells licked dry by predators that will suck the blood from a fat rabbit's throat or savage a nest of newly hatched ducklings in the blink of an eye. This is the law of nature by which we must abide because it means survival for all the different species. We live at the expense of others. This I can accept as the way of the wild, but when man steps in, the wild things don't stand a chance.

On some of my weekend walks with Toby Jug, I would relive my childhood exploits by seeking to discover where the birds had built their nests. Not, I hasten to say, to steal their eggs, but only to observe with awe the ingenuity of a tiny bird in constructing a home for its family. Once we found a blue tit's nest of carefully selected dried grass, deep in the crevice of a tree and holding fifteen minute white eggs covered in orange spots. On another walk we discovered a blackbird's nest of dark olive-green eggs with dusky stripes concealed under a tuft of grass, and also a skylark's nest, an ingenious open-plan construction placed in wide-open landscape and containing three finely shaded eggs. I showed Toby where the nests were, but apart from a casual sniff he did not seem all that interested – he was more interested in birds than eggs.

In winter our walks often took on a very different perspective. For instance, when the trees were bare of leaves it was easier to catch sight of the activities of larger birds such as rooks. It was interesting simply to watch the detailed activity of a rookery. The rooks would steal food from each other, but when any bird thought another's nest looked better than its own, then jealousy was aroused and there would be daylight robbery of nesting material. I was fascinated by the way the rooks would gather in a circle in a field as if they were having a community conference. I never fathomed what was really going on, but I was impressed by their intelligence.

When the first fall of snow came and was followed by a hard frost, a walk out by the river and over the fields would reveal much that was normally concealed. The snow casting a blank sheet over the ground would highlight the burrows where the rural rats nested as lines of humped earth. Game trails of deer and wild boar also became evident as pathways across the land and through the forest.

Toby Jug seemed to enjoy these excursions as much as I did – I could tell by the excitement in his eyes that his basic cat instincts were aroused. He was always mad keen to go with me whenever I chose to go out. Despite snow, wind or rain, he would be there at my side or foraging in front of me.

I liked to go out early enough to catch the sunrise – usually in late spring or the beginning of summer when it was sufficiently warm to entice me from my bed. With Toby Jug on his lead at my side, we would experience what I called the fragrance of dawn. As the first delicate shafts of sunlight touched the land, it would give up the sweet scent of grass freshened by dew and the aroma of the wild flowers as they unfurled; even the trees gave off an intoxicating bouquet of the resins from their bark. Toby and I would often stop, and in union we would sniff the air.

When I thought of the hustle and bustle of city streets, the grinding noise of traffic and loud chatter of humanity in the cafés and on the buses, I felt privileged to live in such a quiet rural setting. One of the most endearing characteristics of my cat was his preference for silence. Toby Jug only miaowed or wailed when he had something serious to say. Even his purrs had a dulcet appeal, but most of the time he preferred the sound of silence.

As well as the dawn, the sunset is a favourite time of day. As daylight begins to fade and the dusk descends over the land, it brings a sense of relief that the business of the day is done. When the sky is clear there is a vivid celebration of colour that can make anyone stop what they are doing for a moment. As the sun sinks towards the horizon there can be bursts of pink and green, with patterns of indigo, red, gold and orange, before a finale of gossamer amber known as the gloaming.

Sometimes Toby Jug and I would go further afield than our immediate surroundings. Alnmouth, a picturesque little village perched on a stretch of land that juts out to sea and lies alongside the winding estuary of the River Aln, provided just the right place for our meandering walks. The views from the seashore were spectacular and the estuarine mudflats, saltmarsh, sand dunes, scrub and the small offshore island were in demand by the wild bird population throughout the seasons. We often observed native birds such as redshank, eider ducks and another large wader, the oystercatcher, in addition to short-eared owls and foraging birds such as the curlew. Toby and I sometimes walked for miles along the coastline, which in parts was reminiscent of our rides with the horse, Lady May.

Following the troubles surrounding the otter hunt that autumn, I wished we could go for more walks together and that I could set aside all other activities and do a spell of watercolour painting, which I had always found therapeutic. The shape and setting of individual trees had always attracted my imagination and I wanted to try and capture the shades of the countryside. At this late time of the year all the deciduous trees put on an elegant show, but some more so than others. The copper beech sheds stunningly colourful leaves of dark reddish brown, while the fallen oak leaves are a subtle gold, but the ash and the sycamore outdo the others with their range of pretty shades of scarlet blush, especially if there has been a late, wet summer. The fantastically wide range of colours on the dying leaves of our native woodlands is wonderful to behold on a walk or ride on horseback through forest glades where the earth is given myriad tints by the carpet of leaves. The full display of gold, cinnamon and russet pink leaf-fall seems to last only momentarily before the first hard frosts turn the ground into a wet, muddy-brown dank mush.

Meanwhile, the turn from autumn to winter is highly significant for wildlife in the struggle to survive. Squirrels and mice feverishly hunt durable food items such as nuts, flower bulbs and eggs to store away for winter. It is a time when the cottage householder can expect rodents to seek a warm berth inside. To avoid such lodgers at Owl Cottage, I had to resort to strong measures. Since I hate to trap and kill creatures, the most effective remedy I found to keep mice and rats at bay was to put down a regular scattering of chilli powder and pepper around the walls and sink outlets. If this didn't deter a mouse, and it successfully took up residence in the cottage, I would use a box trap baited with cheese or chocolate to capture the mouse alive. It is necessary however, as I learned from hard experience, to liberate the intruder at least a mile from the cottage or I could expect it to return to sender.

Towards the end of that autumn, I found I had another set of intruders to deal with in my garden. This time they posed a most serious threat to the health of Toby Jug and me, as well as to my neighbours.

The problem had come to light when I decided that I needed more storage space for my gardening tools, wheelbarrow and lawnmower. The garage was already full to capacity with a small work bench and ladders, so I went to a store in Scotswood in search of a shed. I soon realized that even the smallest flat-packed shed was too large to fit into my Mini so I reluctantly had to pay an excessive amount for delivery. When the item was delivered I had to work out the best way to assemble it, but I am not possessed of effective handyman skills and the new purchase presented me with immense problems of construction.

In desperation, I hired a local joiner to help me. He

constructed the shed whilst I laboured for him and Toby Jug looked on with bemusement. The joiner made things look so simple that I was embarrassed at my own incompetence. He didn't need to read the elaborate book of instructions, and in no time at all I had a spanking-new shed erected on site.

In order to give the shed a hard base I had dug out an oblong patch of soil and laid a concrete footing. This had been my main contribution to the building, but following the erection I discovered that I had unearthed a menacing problem. I had impinged on a previously undetected hornet's nest buried in a disintegrating log deep in the ground. The concrete had overlapped part of the nest and blocked off one of the exits. Of course, the extent of this problem did not emerge until a few days after the project had been completed and the damage was done. The shed was now erected and ready for use, and nothing could be done about that.

All of this came to light when one morning as I stood with my morning cup of tea, gazing across at the Cheviot Hills, when I was attacked by some hornets. I was stung only twice, but that was enough to send me running for shelter before the whole colony came at me. The stings were so severe that I was forced to seek medical attention at the local surgery. The lumps on my arm were inflamed red and extremely painful. My condition called for treatment with antihistamine drugs. Later I was told that hornets have stronger venom in their stings than wasps, and also that an individual hornet can sting many times, unlike bees which lose their sting the first time they use it.

After treatment at the surgery I decided to have a bowl of lentil soup at the Running Fox Café. It was made by Joan, the proprietor, from her own recipe and was just what I desired at that moment. With the soup and a mug of hot creamy coffee inside me I felt quite pleasantly restored and recounted my tale of woe with the hornets to other locals in the café. I was surprised to learn that the hornets were not only a problem in my garden but had become a threat to the whole village.

It was clear that it was incumbent upon me to do something about the hornet's nest for everybody's sake, but what could I do? Getting rid of insect infestations is no easy matter, as I remembered when a swarm of bees invaded the cottage a few years earlier. I was given a great deal of advice, most of which was well intentioned but spurious.

'Pour petrol on the nest and burn them out!'

'Put rat poison in some honey and feed it to them.'

'Dig them out and drown them with spray from a garden hose.'

'Phone the council for the best advice on how to get rid of them.'

I pondered all these suggestions and eventually adopted what seemed to be the wisest advice, which was to consult the regional Beekeepers' Association. Hornets constitute an enormous problem for beekeepers because they can invade a hive and kill all the bees. A jolly-faced member of the beekeepers' club advised me to purchase a particular aerosol spray.

After several abortive attempts under threat from their stings, I eventually succeeded in killing many of the hornets by spraying the nest entrances and exits several times during the hours of darkness when the hornets were in residence and dormant. I repeated the dose over several nights and then, for the *coup de grâce*, I resorted to a personal attack. Dressed in a mountaineer's survival suit, lent to me by a sympathetic policeman friend, and wearing thick gloves and a beekeeper's facial mask, I tackled the gruesome job of digging the nest out.

I was surprised at how deeply imbedded the hornets had managed to bore themselves into the decaying wood. The nature lover in me cringed at the act of destroying the product of their natural ingenuity, but I felt that I had no option. I consoled myself with the thought that I was doing all my neighbours in the village a favour. Part of me hoped that the queen hornet escaped the massacre to build another nest far, far away.

During the crisis, Toby Jug was not in evidence anywhere near the centre of the operations. Usually when I am gardening Toby Jug follows me around like a shadow, but any sign of aggressive bees, wasps or latterly hornets, and my cat would make himself scarce at the double.

The successful annihilation of the hornet nest had an immediate effect on Toby's behaviour. The next morning as I set about putting a protective coat of varnish on the timbers of the new shed, Toby appeared, in nonchalant, investigative style, to inspect the remains of my handiwork. He made a thorough analysis by sniffing and pawing every item of the disintegrated nest that was left. When he had finished, he came and sat near me and positively beamed as if to say well done.

'You see what I had to do to avert the danger and no thanks to you!' I said proudly. This remark was studiously ignored as he decided that he might as well give himself a tongue-wash just to pass the time until lunch. 'Cats are such fastidious creatures,' I muttered to myself as I continued the boring task of varnishing the shed.

When I'd finished the paint job I needed to do some specialist shopping and, to Toby Jug's delight, I allowed him to come with me.

'We might as well go to Rothbury rather than attempt to shop at Alnwick and Morpeth as they are bound to be crowded, it being Saturday,' I said to Toby as if he was bothered where we went as long as he could join me for a trip out.

After buying the provisions for the coming week, I stopped by the newly opened pet store and bought a supply of cat biscuits and a new leather harness and lead for Toby, and some additional 'live' mousetraps for the new shed, which I did not want to become a cosy winter home for field mice. Then I went to my favourite hardware store, which had served me well in the past. Here I needed to buy cement sealant to preserve the concrete floor under the new shed, and I also required some mastic with which I could close off any gaps around the plinth on which the shed was erected. I knew from experience how ingenious insects can be in finding a convenient hole in which to nest, and then how tenacious they can be if they have to be moved. I wanted to avoid any further infestations on my property because I hate having to destroy wild things in any form. Finally, I purchased a large oil lantern, some spare wicks and a can of oil to provide light in the shed when needed.

Later, I bought fish and chips to eat as I parked on the field near the river. This was becoming habitual every time we came to Rothbury, but watching Toby demolish his fish treat with such gusto made me smile with satisfaction as I lingered over my own meal and watched the ducks and the swans on the riverside. I liked Rothbury as it was a quiet, rural town with clean air and attractive views where it was possible to acquire most things a household needs, and the butcher's shop was one of the best in the region.

With the thought that it is never too early to think about preparing for Christmas, I called into the butcher's and ordered a medium-sized turkey and a large joint of silver-side beef to collect a few days before Christmas. We would no doubt indulge in a variety of other specially cooked foods to celebrate the holiday, but I felt that turkey and beef would provide both Toby and me with a yuletide delight.

I drove back to the cottage, taking my time on the winding road to appreciate the late autumn sun shining through the fading, translucent leaves. On the return journey I called at the garden centre on the road into Morpeth to buy a new wheelbarrow and a supply of bird food for the hanging feeders I had in the garden, as well as a couple of extra bird boxes. On the way back I parked by the roadside in order to make a quick sketch of a grove of three slender trees growing in the centre of a field. I had long admired this stand of trees every time I passed this way and I was determined to paint them when I could get round to it. With the sketch completed, it was finally time for us to go home.

Once I reached the cottage I stored all the surplus garden gear from the overcrowded garage into the new shed, together with the wheelbarrow and the bird food. Job well done and the crisis over, it was time to take a rest, draw the curtains and set the log fire for the evening. It was already becoming cooler as the nights were closing in and the season's traditional mists and dampness were preparing the land for the frosts and snow. The wildlife was already aware of this and it pleased me to see the birds enjoying the garden fruits as they stocked up for the privations of winter.

This year I had made the decision to leave the blackberries, the rosehips and some of the apples and pears from my small orchard for the birds, squirrels and other wildlife, whose needs were much greater than mine. An experience I had when I last paid a visit to Etal, a beautiful rural village near the border with Scotland, reinforced my views in this respect. Whilst having a cup of tea and a sandwich in the sheltered garden of the quaint Lavender Café, I was amazed by the number of sparrows hopping around the tables searching for dropped crumbs. This caused a great deal of merriment amongst some of the customers as if the birds were putting on an act for the entertainment of visitors. I wanted to say that these little creatures were on the verge of dying each day from starvation and it was no laughing matter, but I stayed silent because, as the saying goes, 'Where ignorance is bliss it is folly to be wise.'

Bird numbers are decreasing with each passing year

because of human destruction of their habitats by building on green areas, cutting down trees and uprooting hedges. Many farmers are also at fault because of their overuse of insecticides and ploughing every available bit of land, leaving no room for wildlife. Sparrows are amongst the birds most at risk, but starling numbers have also decreased alarmingly. I broke the rest of my sandwich into small pieces and distributed them to the hungry birds.

In this vein of thinking, I had resolved not to select holly with berries on the branches as a yuletide decoration but to leave them for the birds. I also put out another hanging peanut feeder to do my bit for conservation.

It was now time for the Harvest Festival at St Michael's Church, situated up the hill from the river, and I needed to make a contribution. I had plenty of sweet apples from the orchard at the top of the garden and a good supply of a large, light-green variety which are more suitable for cooking. Toby Jug's tree had been especially bountiful with a harvest of luscious 'cookers' this year so I had more than enough to share. I also took along a token batch of vegetables – potatoes, cabbages, tomatoes and spring onions.

The little stone church had been tastefully decorated for the ceremony with an abundance of flowers such as vividly colourful dahlias and chrysanthemums as well as a smattering of delicate end-of-season roses. Baskets, boxes and panniers of fruit and vegetables were decorously stacked around on the steps and on the space in front of the altar, and a mass of lighted candles gave the whole interior of the church an air of grace. When the service was over and all the contributors to the festival had been thanked and communal prayers had been said for the poor, light refreshments were served. I drank a glass of home-made elderberry wine, which was surprisingly good, and I pocketed a piece of home-made cheese to give to Toby Jug. I did not usually buy cheese but I knew he liked it because my mother, who was a cheese addict, fed it to him when he stayed with her during my absences.

All things considered, the Harvest Festival had been a great success and I heard, later that there had been more than sufficient produce this year to supplement the larders of those most needful in the parish.

The festival was a signal that it was time to get the cottage ready for winter. After making the minor repairs to the house, such as tightening up screws that had worked loose and mending a window catch, I turned my attention to the slate on the roof that had to be replaced before the rains came. With everything done and dusted, I had to return to my research thesis, which left little spare time for Toby Jug and me, but I realized that stresses and strains were in imminent danger of overwhelming me. It was a case of 'stop the world, I want to get off', so I determined that I would take a break from the rat race over the next weekend.

Apart from looking after our immediate needs, Toby Jug and I would do nothing except enjoy ourselves. I decided that the best therapy for me was to return to watercolour painting. No writing, no research, no handyman jobs around the cottage: just plain and simple painting for creativity's sake and nothing else.

174

I always found that the preparation for a painting session was as much part of the creative process as the actual painting itself, and helped arouse the right mood. Several water jars needed to be filled, a variety of paint brushes laid out and the paper soaked and dried, ready for painting on. Then when everything was ready, the cushion nest next to my computer must be brought from the study and put at the side of the painting materials. There, Toby Jug would assume pride of place to oversee the whole operation. He insisted on sniffing each brush I opted to use, took a token drink from each of the water jars, even when the water in them was discoloured with paint, and insisted on leaving bite marks on the watercolour pencils I used. The most lovable quality about Toby Jug was his enthusiasm to be involved in whatever I was doing, and I valued that highly. When he was with me I never felt lonely because he was a great companion. Even when there was tranquil silence between us there was still this emotional bond.

I turned the pages of my sketchbook and examined the drawn impressions I had made of landscapes empty of all people and just filled with rolling hills and trees. Each sketch brought back to my mind the mystical affect that the countryside can evoke in me. When I came to paint a scene, I would not be picturing the view in the manner of taking a photograph, but seeking to use the landscape as a medium through which to express my feelings when I first had sight of it. I turned another page and similarly attempted to conjure up the sensations I had when I stood staring aghast at the fearsome power of the sea breaking over harbour walls with surging waves. I could see the panorama around me and recall the emotions that were stimulated by the sights I witnessed. The colours of the paints I used reflected my perceptions of the scene, rather than being purely realistic. My personality responded best to the range of hues in the red, orange and yellow spectrum, and I inclined more towards paintings by J. M. W. Turner and the Impressionists who employed vivid colours in their paintings.

Above all, I loved to paint trees. In my garden there was a tree called a whitebeam – I remember the day I bought it as a young sapling from the local garden centre. I planted it the same afternoon and over the years composted and cared for it until it became a magnificent specimen with a thick trunk and light olive-coloured leaves in spring and summer. When these leaves fell in autumn, they turned purple on one side and a muted silver on the other. I loved that tree in all its different fashions and guises, especially when it flowered in late June. I had sought to capture its beauty many times in my watercolour efforts.

I view each tree of whatever kind as unique and possessed of a spirit which affects how it grows and the shape and colouration of its foliage. I would study the tree and sketch it prior to painting. My tree painting I undertook that day with Toby Jug playing at my side was inspired by the many journeys I made into Morpeth – I could not help noticing, each time I travelled down the A1, a particular pair of trees over to my right. They stood alone in the middle of a farmer's field and had long, willowy trunks with a crown of compact foliage that bespoke of a kind of pine tree. I must have passed them on the road at least fifty times before I took courage, stopped in a byway and strolled across the field to view them up close. They were even more impressive than they looked from the roadside. In close contact with the pair of trees I got the distinct impression of something grand and singularly beautiful in their isolation. They had a kind of spiritual aura and I came away feeling inspired and determined to portray them to the best of my ability; I decided to call my painting *The Lonesome Pines*.

When painting, I would struggle for a long time to seek the essence of a scene, such as how the early morning haze on the green of a meadow looked to the passer-by, because I wished to convey some of my elation to whomever saw my effort. When I painted with my watercolours, I think I was trying to give vent to how I feel about life and the universe, to understand the order of the world. Through painting a landscape, a tree or a roaring, turbulent sea, I would be drawn nearer to the ways of nature. I yearned for nothing less than an intimation of perfection in colour and form, but like everyone else I have to be content with the best I can do.

No matter what was going on that autumn, with the otter hunt, a brick being thrown and angry hornets plaguing both Toby Jug and me, we could focus on what made most sense to us – the natural world. After the painting session, both Toby Jug and I paused for a while in a zone of peaceful contemplation.

The fact that my cat appeared to mirror my emotions seemed to show how much our lives were intertwined and simpatico with each other. It was inspiring to realize that a spell of creative effort could leave us contented and at rest with ourselves for the remainder of the day.

At college in the months running up to Christmas, special events added to the daily workload. The drama and music departments put on special shows; the Royal Shakespeare Company came to the Theatre Royal in Newcastle upon Tyne, so a mandatory visit had to be organized for the students; and every year a folk dance group from Norway put on a performance in their national dress for the college and VIP guests from the community of Alnwick. The organization of these events kept me and other members of staff very busy, so it was difficult to find an evening and a weekend free, and I was often late in getting home.

For a while, Toby Jug and I saw little more of each other than for a brief spell in the late evening, a tired slump into bed at night and a rushed cup of tea in the morning. Arriving outside at the cottage late at night, I would stand and whistle for him. Then my spirits would lift as I heard the tinkle of his bell and then saw him running along the path under the streetlights towards me. He always completed our reunion by leaping onto my shoulder where I could stroke and pet him.

Once inside the cottage, I would make each of us a bedtime treat and I would tell him what I'd been doing. I would also promise to make it up to him the first weekend I was free of work commitments and we would have a special walk or trip by car. This busy life continued for weeks until at last the pace of things settled down and I could relax at home with my cat and get on with my private concerns.

One morning when the demands at college had slackened off, Toby Jug and I were taking it easy in the garden, me with the proverbial cup of tea and Toby still chewing on the remnants of his breakfast, when there was the sound of a piercing shriek from a bird further up the garden. Toby Jug immediately ran to investigate and I followed. We were just in time to see the stunning sight of a sparrowhawk flying off with the body of one of my favourite birds, a spotted woodpecker, in his talons. All that was left of this colourful bird was a ring of feathers where the hawk had plucked the bird.

I was sad at the sight and stood at the spot recalling the numerous times I had been pleased to observe the woodpecker on the peanut-feeders hanging from the apple tree. Toby gave the feathered remains a cursory sniff and then looked up at me as if to say, 'We won't be seeing him again.' I comforted myself with the thought that although I would miss the sight of the woodpecker, sparrowhawks have to live too and it was probably a female bird with a late-fledged family still desperate to feed.

'Perhaps on Sunday we'll have a look-see where this hawk has its nest if you are willing,' I said to Toby, not expecting any response, but knowing that he would love such an expedition. I had in mind that such a bird might well have an eerie somewhere high on the old quarry cliffs at the northern side of Stag Wood. It would be a refreshing jaunt for Toby Jug and me if the fair weather held, and something was about to happen which would make the oncoming winter even more interesting.

SOJOURN WITH A PONY TRAP

I rarely had visitors at the cottage, but this was less due to any design on my part than the fact that any socializing tended to be with my colleagues at the college or in a restaurant or pub. I was therefore surprised to find a stranger on my doorstep one Saturday morning. After a preliminary glance I recognized the man standing there as the Reverend David Martin, who had called on me once before to check on the name of my cat, Toby Jug, who had been attending his church services.

'I hope you will excuse my disturbing you but I have a request to make which you might find acceptable.'

Intrigued by his manner, I invited him inside to join me in a cup of coffee. He readily accepted and was full of praise for the old cottage. He became even more fulsome in his pleasantries at the sight of Toby Jug, who rose from his catnap on the footstool to inspect the guest. After stroking and petting Toby, the Revd Martin smiled across at me and asked if he was right in believing that I liked horses.

'Very much so, but why do you ask?'

He explained at length that he and his wife had booked the holiday of a lifetime to the Holy Land. They had planned to do this for some time but something had always prevented them going until now. He had the Bishop's permission, and a temporary substitute clergyman had been arranged to take on the commitments of his church, but there was a problem he had not resolved. I stared across at him, wondering what on earth he could be expecting from me and what it had to do with horses.

His wife, he explained, kept two ponies to pull a small trap she owned, and she regularly rode out with them around the local country roads. They were her heart's delight and she had tried to find a place for them whilst they were away, but all arrangements had fallen through. I began to feel slightly uncomfortable at this news, suspecting what would come next. He shifted uneasily in his chair and looked over at me in what I thought was desperation.

'Several of my parishioners have volunteered to feed and care for the ponies,' he said, 'but none of them had experience of handling horses, especially buggy riding, and you are my last hope. Would you agree to oversee the care of the two ponies and take them out for a short exercise each week?'

He sank back in his chair, obviously stressed at having to ask a virtual stranger for help.

Meanwhile, Toby Jug had quickly returned to lie on the stool as if to say, 'I'm too busy washing my paws to be involved in this.'

'How long is your holiday?' I asked, beginning to feel a little stressed myself.

'Eight weeks,' he said dryly, afraid that I was going to refuse to help.

'I will need to meet the ponies before I can make a decision, and there are other matters to consider,' I said, not agreeing outright.

'I am prepared to offer you a fee if you will kindly accept.'

I waved my hand in a dismissive gesture. 'Where are these horses kept?' I asked, changing the subject.

'The rectory has large grounds at the rear. They extend right down almost to the river. There are two paddocks, stables and a large loosebox. If you would come and have a look at the ponies, my wife Sarah would be delighted to show you round.'

'I've never driven a horse and trap and I don't know if I can.'

'I believe it's rather easy but I've not tried myself. I must admit that I'm not very good with animals, and horses tend to frighten me. As an added inducement we keep a dozen hens which are very prolific egg layers – another of my parishioners has agreed to see to them, but you are welcome to take as many surplus eggs as you want.'

'Well that certainly is an inducement, isn't it Toby?' I said smiling to the recumbent form lying on the footstool who was ignoring the conversation and now emitting a sonorous snoring sound. 'I'll sleep on it and let you know tomorrow, if that's all right. How long will you be away again?' I asked. 'And when are you leaving?'

'We've planned to leave in ten days' time and we should return in just under eight weeks if our transport arrangements are anything to go by.'

As he walked away along the street I could see from his

slumped shoulders that he was worried that I wouldn't be able to help him.

Inside the cottage I poured myself another coffee as I considered the parson's request. Here we go again, I said to myself. I seemed destined to spend my life with horses. Of course, I could hardly turn the man down, but managing two ponies and driving a horse and trap, what would I be letting myself in for? It all depended on how the ponies responded to me tomorrow. If we don't like each other then it's a no-go, I decided.

Right on cue, Toby Jug started his routine of rubbing against my ankle to remind me that lunchtime had come and gone, and he was hungry.

'How would you like to spend time with a couple of ponies?' I asked.

He beamed back at me as if everything in the world would work out okay if only I'd stop jabbering and get us something to eat.

'You might find yourself riding in a horse and trap. How would that suit you?' I speculated, but Toby Jug had other things on his mind at that moment so I shut up and got on with cooking our lunch.

I called on Revd Martin at 8.30 a.m. the next morning because, with it being Sunday, I knew he'd have church services to conduct. He was overcome with emotion when I confirmed that I would supervise the care of the horses and ensure that they were taken out in the trap and exercised – as long as they accepted me and I was able to handle them easily.

Revd Martin then disappeared into the Rectory and

brought out his wife to meet me. Sarah Martin was a pleasant-looking, middle-aged lady who welcomed me with effusive thanks for agreeing to help. She invited me inside, but I excused myself by saying that I knew they had a busy morning and I'd like to meet the ponies as soon as possible. She agreed enthusiastically and led me round to the back of the house and through a five-barred gate into a paddock where the ponies were grazing on fresh straw.

'Do come and meet my pets,' Sarah Martin said, striding towards the ponies, both of which were a rich dark brown with black manes.

'This is Joshua. He's a gelding and very sweet.' She indicated the slightly larger of the two ponies. 'And here is Jezebel,' she exclaimed, hugging the diminutive mare. She turned towards me with a broad smile and declared, 'Aren't they beautiful? They're six years old and have never been separated from birth onwards. They're trained to the trap and very obedient as long as they are together. In the trap there is a long whip by the driver's seat, but it has never been used and I would prefer that they should not to be whipped under any circumstances!' She glanced at me, searching for a reaction.

Whilst I was in full sympathy with her sentiments, I was little irritated at being instructed in horse management and answered her more harshly than I would have done had she been less dogmatic.

'Only in my wildest imagination have I ever entertained the thought of horse-whipping anything with the possible exception of those who torture animals. Do I make myself clear?' I stated as firmly as I could.

'Certainly,' she said with a relieved smile. 'Then you are just the man to leave in charge of my ponies.'

The terms of engagement having been more or less agreed, I now gave my fullest attention to the ponies. They seemed a delightful pair with big, soft brown eyes. I spoke gently as I stroked each of their muzzles and necks in turn and they responded readily and without flinching at my touch.

'They are obviously accustomed to affection and that suits me fine because it is my style with animals, especially horses,' I said, and I could tell that she was warming to my approach.

'Yes, we have heard that about you, which is why we chose to ask you in the first place. David is so impressed with your cat that he's been trying to persuade me to have one, which we might well do after our holiday.'

Following this exchange I was shown around the stables, the loosebox and the grain store next to the hay shed. On the way back to the house we were joined by Revd Martin who was anxious that I should see his hens. At this stage Sarah Martin took her leave after shaking my hand and letting me know that the relevant keys, together with detailed instructions regarding the horses, would be left with me on the day before they left. I wished her a happy holiday and she departed into the rectory.

Revd Martin strode towards a part of the garden enclosed by a sturdy-looking wooden fence. I walked behind him as he led me through a gate into a yard where there was a hen house and a grassed area surrounded by trees and bushes.

'I like my hens to have space to roam at will during the day as close as I can to how nature intended. At night they have to be shut in to keep them safe from foxes. As I told you yesterday, one of my parishioners, George Harding, will be caring for the hens, but you may have as many eggs as you want. These White Leghorns are prolific layers.'

I smiled and nodded to show my appreciation of his chicken-keeping arrangements and thanked him for the offer of fresh eggs.

'You are indeed welcome and I suggest that you accept a fee of £100 for your services while we are away. It is much less than it would cost us to have the horses stabled elsewhere and we'll be much happier if we know they are safe and secure in their usual home.'

I demurred, but he was adamant that I take the fee, and in the end he made me agree. The money would help to cover some further urgent repairs to the cottage, so I was most grateful. As the morning was advancing rapidly it came as no surprise when Revd Martin had to excuse himself to attend to his clerical duties. Before he left, he expressed his thanks for my services so enthusiastically I feared he would hug me. As I was leaving, Sarah dashed out to the gate and presented me with a bag containing half-a-dozen eggs.

'To see you through the week,' she said. 'I'm playing the organ during service today so I must run,' she called over her shoulder as she vanished inside the rectory.

As I walked along the path to the cottage, who should I meet but Toby Jug? He must have seen where I had gone and decided to come and fetch me.

'We're into horses again,' I said as we walked back together. 'Only this time there are two and lots of hens.' I recalled his run-in with a hen and a cockerel at my friend Jenny's farm when he was a very young cat. Toby paid not the slightest heed to my words, but I knew he was listening and was just miffed at not being taken to meet the Martins. Nothing of vital importance escaped my cat, I concluded, as he padded along beside me.

I had no doubt that I would be prevailed upon to give him a treat once we were back in the cottage to make up for not taking him with me. Like many cats, Toby Jug was devoted to treats. Now and again he would pester me for a treat between meals when I was busy working. I realized that he probably felt hunger pangs and was eager to make me aware of them in no uncertain terms by wailing close to my face.

The quality of the treat was of primary importance. On occasion, the offer of a few small biscuits from a 'cat treats' pack would suffice, but if he knew that I had got some cooked meat in the larder, he would not be content until I had stopped what I was doing and got him some. At times, in line with optimal parental practice, I refused to cooperate and said no. When I did, he would usually withdraw out of my sight, wait ten minutes and try again. If I still declined, he would either disappear in a 'I don't love you anymore' state of huff or start raking the carpet with his claws. In spite of these little tantrums, we got along just fine most of the time and I generally forgave him because he had to endure being left on his own for lengthy periods, and I knew he missed me.

* * *

During the following week I had a day free because the Environmental Studies Staff were arranging field-study trips for all the students and I did not have to be involved. Instead, I had a field-study trip of my own, devised to seek out the nesting site of the sparrowhawk that had killed my woodpecker. I could guess where the nest might be, but we would have to set off early, probably in the dark, to have a good chance of seeing the hawk.

With this in mind it was necessary to be early to bed on Tuesday night so we could rise early on Wednesday. Even though Toby Jug was supposed to be a nocturnal creature he abhorred getting up in the dark. I expect that his conditioning through living with me was responsible for this. Nevertheless, when I rose at 6 a.m. on a cold November morning he joined me in the kitchen. He proceeded to yawn a few times just so that I'd get the message that rising at such an unearthly hour on a chilly wintry morning was beyond the call of duty. But after demolishing a handful of his biscuits he was ready and waiting by the front door as I slipped on his harness and we set off into the darkness.

Since there were no manmade lights where we were walking and the sky was clear, there was a heavenly display of stars sprinkled across the sky. I could not but stop and stare at what most of the population never see because of light pollution.

We didn't need a torch as we skirted the looming mass of Stag Wood and headed along a stream that took us around the forest towards the remains of the old stone quarry. The area below the massive cliff was lined with scrub and bushes, and we stopped for a breather. I had loaded a backpack with a flask of coffee and a meat pie I'd bought from the butcher's in Rothbury. For Toby Jug I'd brought two small slices of cooked pork, also from Rothbury, which I'd cut into bite-size pieces. A small jar of tap water sufficed for Toby's drink and we sat on a large, flat stone to consume our breakfast al fresco and await the dawn.

The stars faded to give way to a brightening with the first rays of dawn light. The stark rock-face of the quarry towered above us, still in shadow until a sliver of sunlight revealed the craggy stone edifice near the top of the soaring cliff. There were furtive movements among the cracks and crannies of the rocks, and through my small pair of binoculars I could discern quite clearly dark-winged flappings as the birds strove to warm themselves after the cold night.

Toby Jug and I watched in fascination as the first birds took flight and, much to Toby's alarm, I whistled in surprise as I identified a pair of peregrine falcons already ascending to a commanding height as they glided in circles over the plain below, waiting for the sun to rouse the songbirds and pigeons roosting there. I scanned the cliff for any signs of the sparrowhawk, but clearly the peregrines dominated the area; as the superior birds of prey, they would be unlikely to share their pitch with other raptors. We may have failed in our mission, but seeing the peregrine falcons in flight was more than recompense.

The rising sun cast long shadows in front of us and

made me even more aware of the morning chill around us. I looked down at Toby and saw him shivering. Time to set off back home for some warmth. As we walked away, I spotted a flock of pigeons taking flight and I guessed that somewhere higher up the peregrines would be sighting their prey prior to the hunt, when they could hurtle downwards at amazing speeds. It was a shame it was too cold to stay any longer. As we headed homewards our feet marked prints in the white rime on the paths.

As we were passing by a woodland copse, a figure emerged from the darkness and hailed me. It was Tom with his dog. He wanted to tell me something.

'Last night I seen otters, a whole family swimming in the pool down by the weir,' he gasped breathlessly. 'Thought you'd like to know.'

'Thanks, Tom. That's great news!'

He waved and was gone, swallowed up in the gloom of the trees.

'Toby, I think we ought to make a detour,' I said, and I changed direction towards the weir on the River Coquet.

I knew the pool Tom had mentioned, but there was no sign of otters when we arrived, just a serene expanse of water undisturbed in the early morning light. 'Of course,' I muttered, 'they'll be sleeping now. Safe and secure in their holt, all cuddled up cosy together in their cavern deep underground.'

The peaceful scene gladdened my heart, knowing that the otters were safe. Toby looked tired so I carried him the rest of the way home and told him how pleased I was to hear the good news from Tom.

*   *   *

I paid another brief visit to the Martins to wish them a happy holiday before they left and I had a quick look once more at the two ponies. I also spent a little time with Sarah Martin to check out how to arrange the harnessing on the small horse carriage, in which the ponies would be arranged side by side. In addition, she told me the verbal commands to which the ponies would respond, advised me how far the horses would normally go on a trip and where best to take them for a run.

After the Martins had gone, I called on the ponies every day to see that all was well. On each visit, I went through my habitual 'getting to know you' routine with horses by giving them treats such as apples and carrots, and giving them tender loving care with strokes and gentle words of comfort.

Joshua, the gelding, did not seem to warm to me at first, whereas Jezebel responded with enthusiasm to my offerings. Neither of the ponies took to Toby Jug initially, but as the weeks progressed the attitudes of the horses gradually improved towards both of us, and by the end of the third week of daily attendance we were all firm friends.

Prior to this stage I had not attempted to ride out in the trap with them, but at least three times a week I walked them individually around the paddock area so that they could have some exercise and also familiarize themselves with me and my voice. Toby Jug declined my efforts to get him to ride on one of the ponies' backs, perhaps because of his fond memories of Lady May, which were still haunting both of us.

The fourth weekend since the Martins had embarked was sunny and fair without the cold winds of the previous weeks, so I decided to harness the ponies into the trap and take a ride. Toby Jug acted dubious at first, but when he saw that I was about to ride off he rapidly changed his mind and jumped up onto the narrow carriage seat beside me. As soon as I softly spoke the first command of 'walk on', the ponies dutifully responded and set off at a pleasant trot. In this way we rattled along the tree-lined country lane towards Longframlington.

Once we reached the main road I took a detour down to Linden Hall where I stopped at the pub and begged a pail of water for the horses, which I allowed to graze on a grass verge. Meanwhile, I ordered a glass of Merlot and a plate of beef sandwiches and sat at one of the outside tables. Toby Jug enjoyed the beef filling from two of my small sandwiches, and then, with everybody rested, watered and fed, we travelled back along the route we had come in wintry sunshine with a cool breeze blowing in our faces.

Everything had gone swimmingly well. After grooming the ponies and giving them some grain and hay, I bedded them down with many words of praise before leaving with Toby.

Whilst the spell of fine weather remained, I made two other trips with the ponies and I began to enjoy sitting behind them as a change from riding on horseback. I relaxed back on the wooden seat, graced with a comfortable cushion, held the reins and watched the world go by at a more stately pace than rushing around in a car.

By the time of the fourth trip in the pony trap I began to feel somewhat aristocratic as if I were back in the time of Jane Austen. The journeys were rather more enjoyable because the gait of the ponies was so less hurried and there were ample opportunities to sit lightly holding the reins while leaving the hard work to the horses. It felt grand to take a relaxed moment to stare at the passing hedgerows, the sheep and the cows in the fields and the majestic trees on our route.

We drove to the harbour and the estuary beach at Amble and I collected driftwood for the cottage fire. I'd also brought some bread and leftover cooked potato for the ever-present seagulls, which descended on the scraps of food with so much screaming and shrieking that it almost unnerved Joshua, who kept pulling at the harness to be on his way. Strangely enough, Jezebel never turned a hair and looked back at me in apparent sympathy, as I fought to control Joshua, as if to say, 'Isn't he a nuisance?' After a while he quietened down as I held his head and stroked his mane. A treat of half an apple each reassured the two ponies that all was well and that they might as well just relax, enjoy the sea air and have a rest before having to make the return journey.

My several excursions with the ponies and trap gave me a little of the tranquil solitude I crave so much, and on each trip I revelled in the delightful company of my favourite animals, my cat and two fine little horses.

The day before the Martins were due to arrive back I made doubly sure that everything was in A1 order. Whatever needed to be rectified I did, and I groomed the ponies until their coats shone like satin. In my role as a general caretaker I left nothing amiss.

When they arrived back, David and Sarah Martin were so pleased that they called to thank me in person and I entertained them with coffee and we exchanged tales of our adventures. They were delighted to hear how much pleasure I had got from the ponies and assured me that I could take them out anytime. As well as the fee I'd earned, they had brought me a present of a litre of Israeli liqueur brandy, purely for medicinal purposes, they said with affectionate winks and smiles. I also thanked them for the supply of fresh eggs, which had provided many breakfast delights. I was invited to attend the talk and slide show of their holiday experiences which Revd Martin had promised to give in the church hall for the local history society.

Since Christmas was close at hand there was much activity at college before the holiday break, and it suddenly occurred to me that another year had slipped by and here I was again needing to plan a Christmas celebration for Toby Jug and myself. I decided that our yuletide feast this year would be less elaborate than last year's, but as well as the turkey and beef I had already ordered, there would be an important addition in the form of some exotic baked breads, which I had read a lot about and was determined to try making. Whilst they would not appeal to Toby Jug's taste, he would join in all the fuss of the preparations and the cooking because he liked to be involved in whatever was going on.

Once I was free of college commitments, I cleared the wooden kitchen table and assembled all I would need for the recipes. For my first effort I chose to bake a batch of cinnamon, apple and raisin bagels.

In a large glass baking bowl I mixed some strong white flour with tablespoonfuls of sugar and salt, a large slice of southern Irish best golden butter, lots of ground cinnamon plus a fresh stick of cinnamon broken into segments, three eating apples from the garden, chopped finely, and a full packet of select raisins. Once water was added to the dish, all the ingredients had to be mixed thoroughly, which was tough going. Then I added a wine glass of rose water and a sachet of dry yeast. Finally, I added a cupful of strong mulled wine to give the bread a festive flavour.

All the while I was mixing the ingredients, Toby Jug sat in his little red hen posture, with his legs tucked under his body, and watched everything I did with avid attention. After mixing, I took the mixture out of the bowl and kneaded it thoroughly. Covering the bowl with a tea towel, I placed it in the refrigerator to settle and rise for an hour, and then put it into the oven for an hour and a half.

Worn out with the effort but pleased at the prospect of fresh-baked bagels, I retired to the sitting room with Toby and sat by the fire with a reviving cup of creamy Irish coffee. To pass the time while the bread was cooking, I played a recording of Mahler's fifth symphony.

Once out of the oven, the bread smelled so delicious that I couldn't resist having one of the buns. Eating fresh warm bread lathered in succulent butter is not a common English tradition, but if the delightful taste I had that night is anything to go by, it jolly well ought to be. The taste was out of this world and well worth the effort. To appease Toby

Jug, who didn't eat bread of any kind, I treated him to a corned beef snack from the fridge so he wouldn't feel left out.

Now I had to set my mind to the final preparations for Christmas. The weather forecast was filled with gloomy predictions of extreme cold and snow. 'What's new?' I thought, but then we were accustomed to that and I was already in the process of ordering more coal and logs to keep us warm.

The turkey and prime beef would soon be available to collect from Rothbury and no doubt I would make the Northumbrian winter broth I had enjoyed last year. I had also stocked a supply of sirloin steaks in the new freezer to keep Toby Jug and me at full strength to cope with the expected storms and blizzards. There would be a new pine tree to decorate with tinsel and baubles and, as always, a multitude of candles to lift our spirits and welcome the New Year. All along, I kept Toby Jug informed of developments. After kindling the logs and closing the curtains, I sat facing the blazing warmth of our fire with Toby Jug alongside me, hugging the best spot.

'Are these arrangements I've mentioned all right with you?' I asked him, wanting to keep my pal in the picture. He looked up at me and seemed contented.

It had been quite a year, with adventures involving horses, otters, hornets and a ghoulish torture chamber, and both of us had disappeared from Owl Cottage for a while – with me lying in hospital and Toby becoming forlorn and hiding away for days in his secret place. He had grown into an adult cat who managed to take everything in his stride.

'Despite the ups and downs, has it been a good year, Toby Jug?' I asked.

To my utter astonishment Toby Jug glanced up at me again, suddenly leapt onto my left shoulder, and began purring and nuzzling my ear. He had made his reply, which to me was as unequivocally positive as the rising of the sun and twice as warm.

PERSPECTIVES

When I decided to write this story of Toby Jug and our life together at Owl Cottage, I wondered where to pick up the threads of my previous *Paw Tracks* books. Looking through my notes and diaries, it soon became clear that 1969 was a definitive time at Owl Cottage and so I chose to focus on just that year. Considered from the viewpoint of where I am now in 2014, as I reach the story's end, I am truly amazed at how much living we did in that single year. I say 'we', of course, because my life would never have been the same without the companionship and the love of my Maine Coon friend, Toby Jug.

When he died in the late seventies, a big part of me died with him, and I was a changed and more mature man because of what he had helped to foster in me. No amount of tears can wash away his place in my consciousness, and I lament his passing almost every day of my life. I have never really been able to get my head around accepting that he has gone. In my dreams I imagine us being reunited and walking together again in some paradise garden. His presence is here with me now as I write this and I will forever miss him.